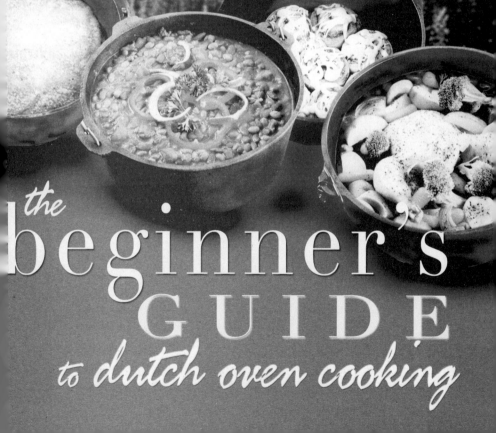

the
beginner's
GUIDE
to dutch oven cooking

Marla Rawlings

the beginner's
GUIDE
to dutch oven cooking

HORIZON PUBLISHERS • SPRINGVILLE, UTAH

ISBN 13: 978-0-88290-688-1
ISBN 10: 0-88290-688-7

Published by Horizon Publishers, an imprint of Cedar Fort, Inc.
2373 W. 700 S., Springville, UT 84663
Distributed by Cedar Fort, Inc. www.cedarfort.com

Printed in the United States of America

10 9 8 7 6 5 4 3 2 1

Printed on acid-free paper

Contents

Introduction

A Little History on the Dutch Oven 11
Seasoning, Re-seasoning and Cleaning Your Dutch Oven . 12
    Seasoning 12
    Cleaning 13
    Re-seasoning. 14
Safety Tips 14
Cooking with Charcoal. 15
Suggested Tools and Supplies 16
Other Suggested Outdoor Cooking Equipment 19
Dutch Oven Environments. 23
    Cooking Indoors with Your Dutch Oven 23
    Dutch Oven Cooking with Outdoor Propane Cookers . . 23
    Campfire Cooking. 23
Oven Sizes and Quantities 24
Other Dutch Oven Tips. 25

1
Great Getting-Started Recipes

Bar-b-Que Stuffed Burgers. 28
Apricot Pork Tenderloin 29
Black Forest Soda Cake 29
Chicken Strips with Honey Mustard. 30
    Chicken 30
    Honey Mustard Dipping Sauce 30
Chuck Wagon Dinner 31
Crazy Crust
Dutch Oven Pizza 32

Dutch Oven
Potatoes Especial 33
Easy Italian Dinner 34
Fast and Easy Cookie Cobbler 34
Hamburger Pie 35
Honey Mustard Pork Chops 35
Hot and Spicy Barbecue Ribs 36
Peppered Onion Biscuits 37
South of the Border Meatball Sandwiches 38

2
Appetizers

Apricot Chicken Wings 40
Dutch Oven Buffalo Wings 40
Dutch Oven Nachos 41
Easy Chili Queso Dip 42
Hot Spinach Dip 43
Hot and Smokey Sausages 44
Hot & Tasty Crab Dip 45
Sweet & Spicy Meatballs 46
   Meatballs 46
   Sauce 46

3
Soups and Stews

Baked Potato Soup 48
Beef Stew with Potato Dumplings 49
   Stew 49
   Potato Dumplings 49
Camping Clam Chowder 50
Easy Chicken Noodle Soup 51
Festive Sausage Soup 52
Five-Alarm Chili 53
One-Alarm Chili 53
Ham & Bean Soup 54

Ham and Broccoli Cheese Soup 55
Hash Brown Soup 56
Italian Meat Ball Soup 57
Short Rib Stew 58

4

Side Dishes

Apple and Squash Bake 60
Broccoli Casserole 60
Hot & Spicy Onion Rings 61
Hot Cocoa Mix 62
Old Fashioned Baked Beans 62
Fried Apples 63
Homemade Root Beer 64
Honey and Spice Carrots 65
Hoppin' John 66
Hush Puppies 67
Southern Corn Casserole 68

5

Breads

Buttermilk Biscuits 70
Cheesy Spoon Bread with Corn 70
Cowboy Cheese Bread 71
Dutch Oven Corn Bread 72
Easy Herb Biscuits 73
Herbed Bread 74
Italian Garlic Bread 75
    Bread 75
    Topping 75
Pizza Crust 76

6
Main Dishes

Barbecue Chicken Pizza 78
Beef Barbecue Sandwich. 79
Barbecue Chicken Deluxe 80
Broccoli and Cheese Rice with Chicken. 81
Cabbage Rolls 82
Cajun Catfish with Horseradish Sauce. 83
   Cat fish. 83
   Horseradish Sauce 83
Chicken and Dumplings 84
   Chicken. 84
   Dumplings 84
Chicken Enchilada Casserole. 85
Chicken Parmesan 86
Chile Relleno Casserole. 87
Curried Turkey with Rice. 88
Corned Beef Dinner 89
Fast and Easy Lasagna 90
Ginger & Orange Steak. 91
Grandma's Pot Roast 92
Honey Lime Ribs 93
Honey Orange Chicken. 94
Italian Style Pizza. 95
Lemon & Dill Cod 96
Meat Lovers' Pizza 97
Meatloaf Dinner. 98
   Meatloaf 98
   Vegetables 98
   Sauce 99
New Potatoes with Peas and Pork 99
Paradise Island Pork 100
Salmon with Lemon and Garlic Butter. 101
Seven Layer Dinner. 102
South of the Border Goulash 103
Spicy Chinese Beef 104

Spicy Pasta Stir Fry 105
Sweet & Spicy Chicken. 106
Turkey and Cornbread Stuffing Dinner 107
Turkey with Herbed Wild Rice 108

7
Breakfasts

Blueberry and Cream Cheese Coffee Cake. 110
Breakfast Hash 110
Breakfast Hash Browns with Bacon 111
Breakfast in a Pot 112
California Quiche 112
German Pancakes Dutch Style 113
One-Pot Breakfast. 114
Sticky Buns 115
Upside Down Apple Cinnamon Rolls 116

8
Desserts

Blueberry Tart 118
Candy Bar Cake. 119
Cherry Apple Crumble 120
Cranberry Apple Cobbler 121
German Chocolate Turtle Cake. 122
Old Fashioned Peach Cobbler 123
    Fruit base 123
    Sweet Biscuit topping 123
Pumpkin Crumble. 124
    Crust and Crumb Topping 124
    Filling 124
Spiced Apple Raisin Crumb Cake 125
Toffee Cake 125
Upside-Down Tropical Delight 126

9
Group Cooking

Cooking for Crowds 128
   Meats 128
   Vegetables 128
   Miscellaneous 129
Beef with Biscuits. 131
Chicken and Potatoes 132
Chili Dogs. 133
Complete Barbecue Dinner. 134
Corn Dogs. 135
Dutch Oven Fajitas 136
   Garnish 136
Easy One-Pot Spaghetti. 137
Hawaiian Pork Chops. 138
One-Pot Spanish Chicken with Rice 139
One-Pot Stroganoff 140
Sloppy Joe's 141
Tacos in a Bowl 142
   Toppings 142

About the Author 143

Introduction

M y purpose in writing this cookbook was to alleviate much of the fear involved in Dutch oven cooking. Dutch oven cooking can be very intimidating to the beginner. We had our first oven for quite a while before we used it because we didn't know how to begin. We found a lot of books on Dutch oven cooking, but we felt overwhelmed by the many instructions that were given and by the many procedures that we thought we were supposed to follow. It all looked so complicated!

I later learned from experience that Dutch oven cooking is easier than I thought it would be, and it's not as complicated as it is made out to be. I discovered that a Dutch oven is very forgiving, and that the best teachers are time and experience, so just relax and enjoy your Dutch oven experience.

A Little History on the Dutch Oven

Dutch ovens were used by pioneers, both in their homes, and as they traveled across America. As the pioneers headed West, women made bread in the morning and placed the dough in the Dutch oven. As they traveled, the bread would rise. At night, when they made camp, they cooked the bread as part of their evening meal. Pioneer camps were filled with ovens hung from tripods over fires, simmering soups or stews, while the breads cooked on the coals below. Pioneers cooked with Dutch ovens because they could prepare a whole meal in one pot, and clean up was easy. The original Dutch ovens were taller and the sides of the pots were steeper. They also had no legs. Adding legs lifted the oven off the coals and made it easier to control the heat on the bottom. Legs also made the oven more stable.

Dutch oven cooking had almost become a lost art, but in the last few decades it has become quite popular with campers, hunters, Boy Scouts, and all outdoor enthusiasts.

Seasoning, Re-seasoning and Cleaning Your Dutch Oven

Ask every Dutch oven cook you know, and chances are each will give you different directions on how to clean, cook in, and care for a Dutch oven. These instructions are simple. Before you season your oven, wash it in very hot soapy water and then rinse well. New cast iron comes from the manufacturer with a wax coating to prevent rusting during warehousing and retailing. Washing will remove the manufacturer's coating and prepare your oven for the seasoning process.

Seasoning

Seasoning in an oven or on an outdoor propane cooker: After washing your Dutch oven, place the lid on top of it and heat in a 350-degree oven for half an hour. Or, place it on a stove top or propane cooker at medium heat until the oven stops smoking. (Use caution when removing the lid of the oven. Never open it towards your face, as heat from the oven may flare out at you.) Remove the oven from the heat and allow it to cool just until it can be easily handled. Wipe off any remaining coating with paper towels. (If the oven is still sticky, heat it again until the sticky coating has burned off.) Pour a little oil or cast-iron conditioner into the bottom of the oven, then spread it with paper towels to coat the entire surface of the oven and lid with a thin coat. Be sure to coat the entire oven inside and out. This must be done while the oven is still very warm. Replace the lid and heat the oven again until it is very hot to the touch. Heating opens the pores of the oven and allows the oil to soak in and create a good seasoning. Let it cool, then wipe any excess oil from oven. Do not leave areas of thick oil, as it may turn rancid and give your Dutch oven a bad taste. If this does happen, follow directions for cleaning and re-seasoning.

Camp fire or charcoal briquettes: Heat the oven until it stops smoking, then follow the above directions. This method carries a greater risk of the oven flaring and creates a lot more ash and soot. I prefer the first method.

Cleaning

Water method: Many people say never to use water to clean your Dutch oven because it may ruin the seasoning. But, if done correctly cleaning with water will maintain your good seasoning. I do not, however, use dish soap. Use soap only if you are trying to remove rust or a bad or rancid flavor. If used often, the soap breaks down the grease and will remove the seasoning you have worked so hard to achieve and maintain. A really good cleaner and conditioner made of a natural soap product can be purchased now, and it cleans very well. Ask an outdoor retailer who sells Dutch ovens if you are interested in this product.

To clean your cast iron oven, wipe off any remaining food and food particles and fill it about half full of warm water or water with cast-iron cleaner. Cover the oven and heat it until the water has loosened any remaining food. Dump the water out and wipe or scrape oven to remove any left-over food. Repeat the water process again if food still remains in the oven. Heat the oven over medium heat until it is very hot and all the water has evaporated. Remove it from the heat and wipe with a thin layer of oil or conditioner. Heat a second time, and wipe all thick spots of oil. Re-heating the oven a second time after it is clean is an optional step. I do it to make sure the pores are open to the oil. It also is a good way to make sure the oil is not too thick.

To store the oven, place a paper towel or rag inside it to absorb any moisture, then prop the lid open slightly with a paper towel that has been folded several times. This will let air circulate into the oven and keep the oven from rusting and the oil from turning rancid.

Dry Clean Method: Some people clean their ovens with salt, newspaper or sand. I do not recommend any of these. Salt promotes oxidization and rust; sand gets trapped in the pores of the oven and will make the next batch of food gritty. As for using newspaper, it just doesn't sound very healthy to clean with something that turns your hands coal black. If you do dry clean your oven, the best way is to scrape any leftover food from the oven, place the lid on tightly and heat until the food has burnt off. Again, never lift the lid towards you. Scrape any leftover particles from inside the oven and heat again, if necessary. Coat it with oil, and store as directed above.

Re-seasoning

Re-seasoning should be done when your oven has not been used for more than a year, has a bad or rancid taste, or has rusted. If your oven has not been used for a long time, clean and season using the water method as directed above. If the oven has a bad flavor or is rancid, use a little soap to remove the bad seasoning. To remove rust spots from your oven, scrub the rust off with a wire-based scrubber and then wash the oven in hot soapy water. Then season it as directed above.

Safety Tips

Dutch ovens become very hot, and caution should be used when handling them. Start fires or coals only in areas that have been designed to contain the fire. Never place or discard coals where they will be stepped on. I have stepped on coals with bare feet before, and it is extremely painful. Thus, my next safety tip is to wear closed-toe shoes to protect your feet from hot ash or coals. Never leave fire or coals unattended. Wear gloves when wiping out or oiling a hot oven, and never place it where children can come in contact with either the hot oven or the coals. Never open an oven toward you. Steam created in the oven can burn your face or hands badly.

Cooking with Charcoal

Cooking with charcoal is a great way to control heat for baking such things as breads and desserts. I have a very simple rule I follow when cooking with charcoal: one briquette equals about 20 to 25 degrees, more or less, depending on conditions. If you are adapting a household recipe and it calls for a 325-degree oven you will need approximately 13 to 17 coals. the chart below will give you cooking temperatures for roasting, baking, or stewing. If conditions are windy, the heat will need to be higher, and the coals will not burn as long. If the outside temperature is cold, the cooking time and/or the number of coals will more than likely need to be increased.

Coals are ready to use when they are mostly gray in color. I suggest using a charcoal starter to prepare coals, and using tongs to place the coals in a checkerboard pattern on top and under the oven. If your cooking time is more than 1 to 1¹/₂ hours, you may need to start an additional batch of briquettes around the end of the first hour to add as the first batch begins to burn out.

Rotate your oven and lid 90 degrees about every 10 to 15 minutes while cooking. This will rotate the hot spots and prevent over-cooking the food in one area.

The following charts compare the number of charcoal briquettes needed for various oven temperatures:

Coals Needed for Various Heat-degree

300 degrees = 12 to 15 coals   400 degrees = 16 to 20 coals
325 degrees = 13 to 17 coals   425 degrees = 17 to 22 coals
350 degrees = 14 to 18 coals   450 degrees = 18 to 23 coals
375 degrees = 15 to 19 coals   475 degrees = 19 to 24 coals

Levels:

Low heat: 250 to 300 degrees, or 10 to 15 coals
Medium heat: 325 to 375 degrees, or 13 to 19 coals
High heat: 400 to 475 degrees, or 16 to 24 coals

Roasting: equal heat on top and underneath
Baking: use a 1-to-3 ratio, with one being the number of coals on the bottom and three being the number on the top. (*Example:* baking at 300 degrees, your would need 5 to 6 coals on the bottom and 8 to 10 on the top; I never use less than 5 coals underneath, as anything less than 5 will result in uneven heat.)
Stewing or Simmering: use a 4-to-1 ratio, with four being the bottom heat and one the top. If you are doing stews or soups with biscuits or dumplings, add more heat to the top when the biscuits are added.
Frying or Boiling: all the heat goes underneath.

Suggested Tools and Supplies

Long-handled tools help you avoid being burned while you're cooking with Dutch ovens. It is important to have a few tools to get started. Then you can add a few others as you go along. Listed below are some suggestions. I have tried to list them in order of importance. You really should have the first five before beginning.

• *Charcoal starter:*
This is a great luxury when cooking with charcoal. Your coals are ready in about half the time and most don't require lighter fluid. There are many on the market. Some can be started over a propane cooker while other are started with newspaper. I suggest you get one with a good sturdy handle.

• *Carrying cases or bags for ovens, handles, lid holders, etc.:*

Utensils, Left-to-right:
Long-handled spatula, 2 ft.; long-handled tongs, 2 ft.;
Long-handled meat fork, 2 ft.; long-handled basting brush, 2 ft.;
long-handled knife, 2 ft.; serving spoon, 1 ft.; slotted spoon, 1 ft.

These are great to store your oven and other supplies in. They will keep soot that is still on the oven from getting on other supplies and protect the oven while storing. A wide variety of bags and carrying cases are available, in all price ranges.

• *Wide paint brush or small whisk broom:*
These are used to brush ashes off the oven lid when you are ready to serve, or to brush ashes off the entire Dutch oven when you start the cleaning process.

• *Lid holder:*
These are usually made to fold for easy storage. They are used to hold your lid while you stir or check the food during the cooking process. Do not place the lid on the ground while cooking—moisture from the hot lid will hold dirt particles on the lid.

Shown below are some of the equipment items that make Dutch oven cooking more enjoyable:

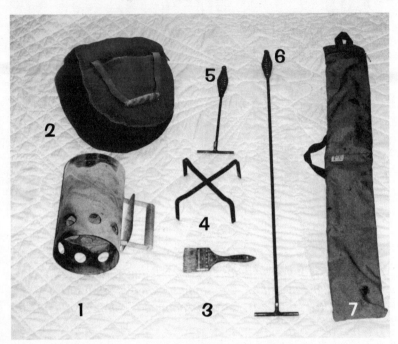

Equipment:

1. Charcoal starter
2. Dutch oven carrying bag
3. Paint brush
4. Lid holder
5. Small lid-lifter, $1\frac{1}{2}$ ft.
6. Large lid-lifter, $2\frac{1}{2}$ ft.
7. Carrying bag for items 4-6

When you put your lid back on the oven the dirt will be released into your food.

• **Handle or lid lifter:**

Lid-lifters are handy for placing on and removing the Dutch oven from the heat source, and also for lifting and rotating the Dutch oven's lid while cooking. This is probably your most important investment. I suggest you get a very sturdy one with a lid stabilizer. The stabilizer will keep your lid from tipping, and that will prevent ashes from getting into your food. It also will allow you to dump ashes from the lid before serving the food.

• *Gloves:*

Invest in a good pair of thick leather gloves. These will keep you from getting burned while cleaning and oiling your Dutch oven.

• *Tongs:*

A long pair of tongs is great for positioning coals on the top and under your oven. Yo may also want a second pair for turning meat while cooking.

• *Cook box:*

I use a large plastic storage box with a lid I store everything I need to cook Dutch-oven style in it, from the ovens themselves to charcoal, to utensils, oil, matches, paper towels, and a few

Other Suggested Outdoor Cooking Equipment

You may want to acquire and use some of these other items along with your regular Dutch oven cooking materials to give variety to your outdoor cooking. The items shown are distributed by Camp Chef, in Logan, Utah.

The Ultimate Dutch Oven uses convection-air-style cooking.
It has separating grids so several dishes
can be cooked at the same time, in less time.

The deep fry turkey pot.

The steel griddle.

The stir fry wok.

The 32-quart stock pot with basket.

*The
Sport
Grill.*

*The
deep fry
pot.*

good cook books. With everything stored in a good cook box, you know you will have everything you need to tackle your next Dutch oven project.

Dutch Oven Environments

Cooking Indoors with Your Dutch Oven

Anything you can cook outdoors in a Dutch oven can be done inside on your stovetop or in your oven. Follow the same directions for temperature and time. **Note:** *Do not use charcoal in your house or RV. The fumes from charcoal are lethal.* Using charcoal is unnecessary if you are baking with your Dutch oven in the oven because the heat will already be evenly distributed. If you are cooking indoors, a Dutch oven without legs works best. The legs sometimes scratch the stovetop surface and may make it a little awkward to place it in and out of the oven.

Dutch Oven Cooking with Outdoor Propane Cookers

This is by far the easiest way to Dutch oven. It is cleaner and more convenient, and can be accomplished at a better cooking level (no bending over hot fires or coals). However, it does lack some of the charm of cooking with coals or over a campfire—you lose a little of the pioneer Dutch oven spirit but you gain a lot of versatility and ease. Outdoor propane cookers cook a lot faster than coals, and are great for areas that don't allow open fires, for tailgating, or for cooking on the beach. Make sure to buy a high quality cooker with stable legs. When using propane, keep your heat to low or medium. If you are doing bread or something that needs to be browned on top, you will need to place coals on top of your oven. A new style of Dutch oven, now available, has a cone-shaped center, comes in several sizes, and has been specifically designed for propane outdoor cookers.

Campfire Cooking

One feels a certain nostalgic charm about cooking over a campfire. The crackle and pop of the fire and the smell of smoke make you step back in time a bit. Cooking Dutch oven-style with a campfire requires a little more guesswork than cooking with coals or propane, and it takes a little practice and experience.

To cook over a campfire, start your fire at least ½ hour in advance. If you are using larger pieces of wood, you will need to allow extra time for the coals to be ready. Maintain the fire, and replenish the coals that burn off. If the fire pit is large enough, you can maintain a fire on one side and cook on the other. If there is no room to do this, prepare a separate pit or area to cook in. Keep your replenishing fire small if it is close to the Dutch oven, otherwise you risk burning your meal with the extra heat generated by the fire. Use a shovel to place coals on and below the oven, then move them into their final positions with tongs.

Oven Sizes and Quantities

These amounts are for ovens that are filled with food:

Size	Holds	Feeds Number of People (approx.)
8-inch	2 quarts	4 to 6 main dish, 8 to 10 side dish
10-inch	4 quarts	8 to 10 main dish, 12 to 14 side dish
12-inch	6 quarts	12 to 14 main dish, 16 to 24 side dish (most common size)
14-inch	8 quarts	16 to 20 main dish, 22 to 30 side dish
16-inch	12 quarts	25 to 30 main dish, 33 to 40 side dish

Most of the recipes in this book can be prepared in a 12-inch oven, unless otherwise stated. When cooking desserts or breads where one layer of food does not fill the oven to the top, the number of servings will be about ½ to ¾ of what is listed above. *Example:* A 12-inch oven would yield about 8 to 10 servings of bread or dessert.

Other Dutch Oven Tips

☞ Make sure your Dutch oven is level when cooking. To do this you may need to prop up one side of the oven with a rock or large coal.

☞ Never add cold liquid to a hot Dutch oven. This can crack your oven.

☞ Never store food in your oven, or store the oven dirty. This will promote rust. It is best to clean the oven as soon as possible after using.

☞ Take extra care not to get ashes in your food. Aspen has an especially bitter taste and will likely ruin your meal. If you are cooking in windy conditions, make sure you remove the lid with the wind, not against it.

☞ Rotate your lid and oven about 90 degrees, every 10 to 15 minutes when cooking. This is a very important step, especially with breads and desserts. Some dishes such as stews and soups do not require rotation.

☞ When you place your lid on the oven, turn it back and forth slightly to make sure you have a tight fit. This will keep moisture and heat from escaping.

☞ If you are cooking several dishes, ovens may be stacked on top of each other. Place the largest oven on the bottom and put a layer of coals between the ovens.

☞ After deep-frying in your oven, strain the oil through a shortening cone when cool. It can then be used over and over again. Use a thermometer and keep oil at a temperature between 325 and 375 degrees. Lower temperatures make food greasy; higher temperatures may lead to spontaneous combustion, especially temperatures over 400 degrees. If the oil is smoking, it is too hot—remove it from the heat and allow it to cool before cooking in it.

☞ For easy clean-up, line the oven with foil before cooking, then simply throw foil away and wipe out the oven. However, unless I am doing a dessert that I want to remove from the oven, I rarely do this. Why? It eliminates the special Dutch oven flavor. The flavor the food absorbs from the oven is one of the reasons Dutch oven cooking tastes so good.

☞ The Dutch oven lid can be placed on coals and the sides of it propped up with rocks or bricks. With this preparation, you can fry on the inside of the lid.

☞ Peeking while your meal is cooking is okay. Half the fun of Dutch oven cooking is to watch the whole process. However, if you peek too much you may increase your cooking time.

☞ Relax and enjoy the experience of cooking the way your ancestors did. It's fun!

Section One

Great Getting-started Recipes

Bar-b-Que Stuffed Burgers

1   lb. ground beef
4   thick slices of cheese of your choice:
    jalapeño jack, Swiss, cheddar or mozzarella
1   cup barbecue sauce
1   onion, sliced
Hamburger buns

Divide the ground beef into four balls. Split each ball into two pieces, then form into patties. Place one slice of cheese between the patties and seal the edges of the ground beef to enclose the cheese. Fry in Dutch oven with bottom heat at 375°, using 15 to 19 coals, until hamburgers are browned on both sides. Place sliced onion on the hamburgers, then pour barbeque sauce over the top. Cover and cook moving coals to a half-and-half ratio for 15 minutes. Serve on toasted buns, adding more barbecue sauce on top of the burgers. *Serves four.*

☞ *Variation:* use mozzarella cheese and cover with tomato-based spaghetti sauce.

Apricot Pork Tenderloin

2   lbs. pork tenderloin   1   cup chicken broth
10 oz. jar apricot preserves   Salt, pepper and garlic
3   Tbsp. vinegar   powder to taste

Season the pork loin with salt, pepper and garlic, then brown it in the Dutch oven with a small amount of oil until the outside of the loin is well browned. Mix together the preserves, vinegar and chicken broth, then pour over the top of the meat. Cover and cook, using 16 to 19 coals (375°) with 1 (bottom)-to-2 (top) ratio for 1 to 1½ hours or until the internal temperature reaches 155 degrees. Add more liquid if needed. Baste or rotate the meat while cooking. *Serves 8.*

Black Forest Soda Cake

2   cans cherry pie filling   1   can cola-flavored soda
1   devils food cake mix   1   cup chocolate chips

Oil the Dutch oven, then pour the cherry pie filling into the bottom of the oven. Place half of the dry cake mix over the top of the cherries and sprinkle on the chocolate chips. Cover with the remaining cake mix, then pour the can of cola over the top. Using a wooden spoon, carefully calm the foam, but do not stir. Cook with 16 to 20 coals (400°) at a 1 (bottom)-to-3 (top) ratio for 25 to 35 minutes. Rotate the lid and oven while cooking. Serve with whipped cream or ice cream. *Serves 8 to 10.*

Chicken Strips with Honey Mustard

Chicken

2   lb. chicken strips or boneless skinless chicken breasts cut into strips or chunks
1   cup flour
$^1/_2$ tsp. salt
$^1/_2$ tsp. seasoning salt
Pepper to taste
$^3/_4$ cup milk
Oil for frying

Mix the flour and seasonings together in one bowl; pour the milk in another. Pour about $^1/_2$ inch of oil into the bottom of the Dutch oven. Heat the oil with bottom heat only, until it is about 325 to 375 degrees. This will take about 16 to 18 coals. Dip the strips of chicken into milk, then roll them in seasoned flour. Cook for about 3 minutes on each side, cooking several at a time and adding more oil if needed. When the chicken is done, remove it from the oven and drain it on a paper towel. Serve hot with Honey Mustard Dipping Sauce. *Serves 6 to 8.*

Honey Mustard Dipping Sauce

☞ This is best if made a day in advance. Mix together
$^1/_2$ cup honey
$^1/_2$ cup mayonnaise
$^1/_4$ cup Dijon mustard

Chuck Wagon Dinner

1½ lbs. ground beef
1   onion, diced
1   can of kidney beans
1   can of whole-kernel corn
1   can pinto beans
3   8 oz cans tomato sauce
2   cups uncooked macaroni
3   cups water or beef broth
1   tsp. each of chili powder,
     ground oregano, and ground basil
Salt and pepper to taste
Grated cheddar cheese

Brown the ground beef in the Dutch oven with onion. Stir in the rest of the ingredients, except the cheese. Cover and cook with 17 to 22 coals (425°), with 1 (bottom)-to-3 (top) ratio for 25 to 30 minutes or until the macaroni is tender. Stir occasionally, and add more moisture if needed. When done, sprinkle cheese on top and cook until the cheese is melted. *Serves 8 to 12.*

Crazy Crust Dutch Oven Pizza

1½ lbs. ground beef
1   clove of garlic, minced
1½ cups flour
1   tsp. Italian seasoning
½   tsp. salt
1   tsp. baking powder
1   cup milk
2   eggs
½   onion, sliced thin
½   green pepper, sliced thin
1   small can sliced olives
1   can sliced mushrooms
1   small jar pizza sauce
2   cups mozzarella cheese

Brown the ground beef with garlic over medium heat. Mix the flour, eggs, Italian seasoning, salt, baking powder and milk together until well blended. Spread browned ground beef evenly over the bottom of the Dutch oven, then pour egg and milk mixture over the top of the ground beef, distributing the batter evenly. Cover and bake with 17 to 22 coals (425°) with a 1 (bottom)-to-3 (top) ratio for 20 to 25 minutes. Top with sauce, cheese, and vegetables, then cook an additional 15 to 20 minutes. Rotate the oven and lid while cooking, and check often. *Serves 4 to 6.*

Dutch Oven
Potatoes Especial

☞ *This is a little bit of twist on the standard Dutch oven potatoes.*

10   large potatoes, sliced, with or without skins
2   onions, sliced
1   lb. bacon
1   green pepper, diced (optional)
2   cups carrots, sliced
1   small package sliced pepperoni
2   cups cheddar cheese, grated
1   cube butter
2   cans of soda pop
Salt, pepper, garlic powder and seasoning salt to taste

Cook the bacon in the Dutch oven until crisp, then remove and crumble it, leaving the bacon grease in oven. Layer potatoes, seasonings, crumbled bacon, onions, green peppers, carrots, pepperoni, cheese, then pats of butter in that order, until everything is used. (This will make about 3 layers, so divide the food into three's as you layer.) Pour one can of soda over the top, then cover and cook, using 16 to 19 coals (375°) with a 1 (bottom)-to-2 (top) ratio, for 40 to 50 minutes. Do not stir while cooking. Add the additional can of soda if needed. Do not let all of the moisture evaporate. Check occasionally while cooking. *Serves 8 to 10.*

Easy Italian Dinner

Brown the ground beef with onion and garlic at 400°, using 17 to 22 coals. Stir in the rest of the ingredients, except for the

1½	lbs. ground beef	1	cup water
1	onion, diced	½	tsp. ea. of ground basil,
2	cloves of minced garlic		ground oregano,
2	jars of spaghetti sauce		cinnamon, and
10	oz. dry spiral pasta noodles		ground red pepper
1	lb. sliced mushrooms	2	cups grated
1	can sliced olives		mozzarella cheese

mozzarella. Cover and cook, moving coals to 1 (bottom)-to-2 (top) ratio, for 25 to 35 minutes. Rotate the lid and oven while cooking. Add more water if needed, and stir occasionally. When the noodles are tender, sprinkle cheese on top of them. Cover them briefly, until melted. *Serves 6 to 8.*

Fast and Easy
Cookie Cobbler

1	20-oz package refrigerator sugar cookie dough
2	cans any flavor pie filling

Pour the pie filling into the oiled Dutch oven, then slice the cookie dough and place it on top of the filling. Cover and cook with 16 to 22 coals (400°) for 30 to 40 minutes. Rotate the lid and oven while cooking and check often. *Serves 8 to 10.*

Hamburger Pie

2 lbs. ground beef
1 onion, diced
2 cans tomato soup
4 to 5 cups mashed potatoes
  (instant potatoes work
  great when camping)

2 cans green beans
2 cups grated cheddar
  cheese
1½ tsp. chili powder
Salt, pepper and garlic
  powder to taste

Season the hamburger with salt, pepper, and garlic powder, then brown it with onion in the Dutch oven at 400°, using 16 to 20 coals with bottom heat only. When the meat is browned, stir in the soup and beans. Spread potatoes over the top of the hamburger mixture, then sprinkle with cheese. Cover and cook moving coals to a 1 (bottom)-to-2 (top) ratio for 18 to 20 minutes, or until everything is hot and the cheese is melted. Rotate the lid and oven while cooking. *Serves 6 to 8.*

Honey Mustard Pork Chops

8 to 10 pork chops
¼ cup Dijon mustard
½ cup of honey
1 Tbsp. liquid smoke

½ cup melted butter
½ tsp. garlic powder
½ cup broth (chicken or pork)
½ tsp. salt

Brown the pork chops in the Dutch oven at 400°, using 16 to 20 coals with bottom heat only. A little oil may be needed. Mix together the rest of the ingredients until well blended. When the chops are browned, pour sauce over the top and cook moving coals to 1 (bottom)-to-3 (top) ratio, for 25 to 30 minutes or until the chops are tender. Add more broth if needed while cooking. *Serves 4 to 6.*

Hot and Spicy Barbecue Ribs

3 to 4 lbs. of boneless pork ribs
1   cup ketchup
1   diced onion
2   Tbsp. mustard
1   Tbsp. liquid smoke
3   Tbsp. hot sauce
$^1/_4$ to $^1/_2$ tsp. ground red pepper
2   Tbsp. Worcestershire sauce
$^1/_4$ cup brown sugar
2   Tbsp. cider vinegar

Brown the ribs in the Dutch oven with a little oil. While the ribs are browning, mix the rest of the ingredients into a saucepan or small Dutch oven. Cook the mixture until it boils, then boil for 5 minutes. Pour the sauce over the ribs, cover and cook with 18 to 23 coals (425°), with a 1 (bottom)-to-3 (top) ratio, for 45 minutes to 1 hour, or until the ribs are very tender. Rotate the oven and lid while cooking, and rotate or stir the ribs occasionally. *Serves 6 to 8.*

Peppered Onion Biscuits

1   package grand-sized refrigerator buttermilk biscuits
1   clove minced garlic
$^1/_2$ tsp. coarse ground pepper
1   Tbsp. dried onion
$^1/_2$ cup butter

Heat the butter with onion, garlic, and pepper in a sauce pan or small Dutch oven until the butter starts to boil. (Take care not to burn the butter.) Place biscuits in the oiled Dutch oven, then brush the butter mixture over the top of the biscuits. If desired, drizzle any remaining butter mixture over the top of the biscuits. Cover and cook with 16 to 20 coals (400°), with a 1 (bottom)-to-3 (top) ratio, for 18 to 25 minutes or until the biscuits are done. Rotate the oven and lid while cooking. *Serves 6 to 8.*

South of the Border Meatball Sandwiches

☞ *These are a tasty alternative to your everyday sandwich.*

4	8-oz. cans of tomato sauce	1	Tbsp. chili powder
1	lb. ground beef	½	tsp. salt
½	lb. spicy Spanish-style ground sausage	1	clove garlic, minced
1	egg, beaten	1	package enchilada sauce mix
¾	cup of cornmeal		Large flour tortillas
1	Tbsp. cumin		

Top with:
Sour cream
Lettuce
Tomatoes
Grated Monterey Jack cheese

Mix together with 1½ cans of the tomato sauce everything but the enchilada sauce mix and the large four tortillas, and mix until well blended. Shape the meat mixture into small-sized balls, then fry them in the Dutch oven, using 15 to 19 coals (375°) with bottom heat only. While the meatballs are cooking, mix the remaining tomato sauce with the enchilada sauce mix and cook it in a small pan until thickened. When the meatballs are well browned, pour the sauce over the top, then cover and cook, moving the coals to a 1-on-bottom 3-on-top ratio, for 15 to 20 minutes. To serve, spoon the meatballs and sauce into tortillas, then top them with desired toppings, roll up and serve. *Serves 4 to 6.*

Section Two

Appetizers

Apricot Chicken Wings

2 to 3 lbs. of chicken wings
Oil for browning
1¼ cup apricot jam
1   package dry onion soup mix
½   cup Russian salad dressing
1   tsp. curry powder
½   tsp. garlic powder

Brown the chicken wings in the Dutch oven with oil, cooking them in batches until all the wings are browned. When the wings are done, return all of the wings to the oven. Mix the remaining ingredients together, then pour them over the top of the chicken wings. Cover and cook with 17 to 22 coals (425°), with a 1 (bottom)-to-2 (top) ratio, for 40 to 45 minutes. Stir occasionally while cooking. *Makes 8 to 12 appetizer servings.*

Dutch Oven Buffalo Wings

2 to 3 lbs. chicken wings
6   oz. hot sauce
½   cup melted butter
Oil for deep frying wings

With bottom heat only, heat the oil in the Dutch oven to temperature between 325 to 375 degrees. Fry the wings a few at a time until they are very crispy. When all of the wings have been cooked, mix the hot sauce and butter together, then toss with the wings to coat them. Serve with blue cheese or ranch dressing. *Serves 8 to 12.*

Dutch Oven Nachos

☞ *These make a great late-night camping snack. I have no exact measurements for this recipe. Quantities depend on how many you are cooking for and how much of each topping wanted on the nachos.*

Use any or all of the toppings listed below:
Tortilla chips
Grated cheese (jalapeño jack with a little cheddar
    works best)
Sliced olives
Diced tomatoes
Browned hamburger or taco meat
Chili
Jalapeño peppers
Refried beans
Green onions

Place a layer of tortilla chips in the oven, then cover them with cheese and desired toppings. For a large batch, repeat this process until the oven is full. **Note:** It is best not to put salsa on chips before cooking—it makes the chips soggy. Using about 18 coals (375°), cook with half heat on bottom and half on top for about 15 minutes, or until the cheese is melted and the toppings are hot. Serve hot with your choice of the toppings listed below.
☞ *Top with*:
Sour cream
Salsa
Guacamole

Easy Chili Queso Dip

☞ *The heat from the oven will keep this dip hot while everyone enjoys it. This recipe makes a large batch that serves many people. To make a smaller batch, use a small package of cheese and one can of chili.*

1   large package of processed cheese
2   cans of chili con carne
Hot sauce to taste

Cut the processed cheese into large cubes and place them in a 10-inch Dutch oven or slow cooker. Pour the chili over the top and add a few dashes of hot sauce. Cover and cook at low heat, using 8 to 10 coals (275°) with the half-and-half ratio. Rotate the oven and lid while cooking, and stir to help melt the cheese. When the cheese is melted, add more hot sauce, if desired, and serve hot with tortilla chips or crackers.

Hot Spinach Dip

☞ *This is a great appetizer.*

1   9-oz. package of spinach
¼   cup diced green onions
1 to 2 cloves of pressed garlic
½   cup crumbled feta cheese
½   cup mayonnaise
1   cup cheddar cheese
½   cup sour cream

☞ *Serve with any or all of the following:*
Crackers
Melba toast
Crusty toasted garlic bread

Thaw and drain the spinach, then chop it into small pieces. Mix together all of the dip ingredients and spread them into a 10-inch Dutch oven. Using 14 to 15 coals bake at medium heat (300°), with 1 (bottom)-to-3 (top) ratio, for about 12 to 15 minutes. Serve as a dip, or spread it on bread and/or crackers. *Serves 8 to 12.*

Hot and Smokey Sausages

2   lbs. small smoked sausage links
1   8 oz. bottle Russian dressing
1   cup grape jelly
¼   cup hot sauce
3   Tbsp. liquid smoke
½   cup brown sugar

Mix together everything but the sausages until well blended. Cook the sausages in the Dutch oven for a few minutes (this releases some of the juices in the sausage and adds a little more flavor to the sauce). Pour the sauce over the top of the sausages, then cover and cook, using 16 to 20 coals (400°), with a 1 (bottom)-to-2 (top) ratio, for 20 to 25 minutes. Stir occasionally while cooking. *Serves 8 to 12.*

Hot & Tasty Crab Dip

☞ *This is great appetizer that everyone can snack on while they are waiting for the rest of their meal.*

2   packages of softened cream cheese
2   6 oz. cans of crab meat (drain and reserve the juice)
$\frac{1}{2}$ cup finely diced green onion
1   cup grated cheddar cheese
$\frac{1}{2}$ tsp. lemon juice
$\frac{1}{2}$ tsp. lemon pepper
Dash or two of Worcestershire sauce
$\frac{1}{2}$ tsp. garlic powder
$\frac{1}{4}$ tsp. curry powder
$\frac{1}{2}$ tsp. salt
$\frac{1}{2}$ to 1 tsp. hot sauce
$\frac{1}{2}$ cup juice from crab
$\frac{1}{2}$ cup milk (or just enough to make dip mixable)

Mix everything together until well blended, adding enough milk to make it easy to blend the ingredients. Cover and cook in a 10-inch Dutch oven, using 14 to 18 coals (350°), with a 1 (bottom)-to-3 (top) ratio, for 12 to 16 minutes or until the mixture is hot. Serve with vegetables, crackers, or crusty bread. *Serves 8 to 12.*

Sweet & Spicy Meatballs

Meatballs

2	lbs. hamburger
2	eggs, slightly beaten
1	onion, diced fine
$1/2$	tsp. salt
$1/2$	tsp. pepper
$3/4$	cup brad crumbs

Mix the egg, onion, bread crumbs and seasonings together, then add the hamburger and mix well with your hands. Form small meatballs, about golf-ball size, out of the mixture. Cook over bottom heat only using 16 to 20 coals (400°), until well browned. Cook several meatballs at a time, removing them when done. When all of the meatballs are browned, drain any left-over grease from the oven. Return the meatballs to the Dutch oven and cover them with sauce (below).

Sauce

1	12-oz. jar of grape jelly
1	12-oz. jar of chili sauce

Juice of one lemon
$1/2$ to 1 tsp. hot sauce

Mix the sauce ingredients together, then pour over the meatballs. Cover and simmer with medium bottom heat for about 20 to 25 minutes. Stir occasionally while cooking. Serve as an appetizer, or make the meatballs larger and serve them over rice as a main dish. *Serves 8 to 12.*

Section Three

Soups and Stews

Baked Potato Soup

5   baked potatoes, diced
1   onion, diced
2   stalks of celery
1   small cluster of broccoli flowerets, cut into pieces
1/2 lb. bacon, diced
2   cups chicken broth
4   cups milk
2   tsp. salt
1/2 tsp. pepper
1/2 cup flour
1   tsp. season-all
1 1/2 cups sour cream

☞ *Top with:*
grated cheese
diced chives or green onions
additional crisp bacon bits

Cook the bacon in the Dutch oven with bottom heat only until crisp, then add celery and onion and cook until tender. Do not drain the bacon grease from the oven. Combine one cup of milk with the flour using a shaker or a wire whisk, and mix until smooth. Add the broccoli to the oven, then stir in the chicken broth, season-all, salt and pepper. Cover and cook with 14 to 19 coals (375°) until the broccoli is tender, stirring occasionally. Slowly stir in the milk, potatoes, and milk-and-flour mixture; cook until the flour has thickened the soup. Stir in the sour cream just before serving, then top with cheese, bacon, and chives. *Serves 6 to 8.*

Beef Stew with Potato Dumplings

Stew

1	lb. beef stew meat	2	cups cabbage, sliced and chopped into pieces
1	large onion, diced		
3	stalks celery, sliced	2	Tbsp. flour
3	large carrots, sliced		3 to 4 cups beef broth or water
3	potatoes, diced		Salt and pepper to taste
1	cup fresh or frozen peas		Oil or bacon grease for
1	cup fresh, frozen or canned corn		cooking the meat

With 16 to 20 coals (400°), using bottom heat only, brown the meat with a small amount of oil in the Dutch oven. When browned, add the onion and cook until the onion is tender. Sprinkle the meat and onion with flour and let it cook a few minutes more, then add the beef broth, celery, potato, carrots and salt and pepper to taste. Cover and cook with 17 to 22 coals (425°), with half the coals on top and half underneath, for about 45 minutes to 1 hour, stirring occasionally and rotating the oven and lid. When the meat is very tender, add the rest of the ingredients and cook them until all the vegetables are tender. Add more broth, if needed. While the stew is cooking, prepare the dumplings recipe.

Potato Dumplings

2	cups shredded potato	1	Tbsp. flour
1	Tbsp. diced onion	$^1/_2$	tsp. salt
1	egg		Dash or two of pepper
$^3/_4$	cup bread crumbs		

Combine the egg and breadcrumbs, and mix well to soften the breadcrumbs. Add onion, flour, salt and pepper. Mix in the potatoes, then form into small balls (about golf-ball size). Roll the dumplings in flour and set them aside until the stew is done. To cook the dumplings, drop them into the boiling stew after the vegetables are tender. Change coals to 1 (bottom)-to-3 (top) ratio, then cover and cook for approximately 20 to 25 minutes or until dumplings are done. Do not lift the lid for the first 20 minutes. *Serves 10 to 12.*

Camping Clam Chowder

2   6$\frac{1}{2}$-oz. cans of minced clams
1   medium onion, diced fine
3   stalks of celery, sliced
3   cups of diced potatoes
3   carrots, sliced thin
$\frac{3}{4}$ cup flour
$\frac{1}{2}$ cup butter (not margarine)
1   quart of half-and-half
1$\frac{1}{2}$ tsp. salt
Pepper to taste

Drain the juice from the clams into the Dutch oven, then add the vegetables. Salt and add just enough water to cover. Cover and cook with bottom heat only, using 14 to 19 coals (375°), until the vegetables are tender. While the vegetables are cooking, mix 1$\frac{1}{2}$ cups of the half-and-half with the flour and blend well in a shaker or with a wire whip until smooth. Set aside. When the vegetables are tender, stir in the remaining half-and-half, butter and the clams. Stir in the flour and half-and-half mixture. Cook until the flour is cooked and the soup is thick, then season with salt and pepper, if needed. *Serves 6 to 8.*

Easy Chicken Noodle Soup

3   cups cooked chicken, cut into cubes
4   large carrots, sliced
1   large onion, diced
4   stalks of celery, sliced
1   quart of chicken stock
Salt and pepper to taste
6 to 10 oz. of homemade egg noodles or frozen wide
     noodles; adjust quantity according to taste.

Place everything except the noodles in the Dutch oven, then cover and cook with 16 to 20 coals (400°) for 20 to 25 minutes, or until the vegetables are tender. Add more chicken stock or water if needed, then bring the soup to a boil. Add noodles to the boiling soup, then cover and cook until tender. Add more water or chicken stock to taste. *Serves 6 to 8.*

Festive Sausage Soup

$^1/_2$ lb. spicy pork sausage
$^1/_2$ lb. hamburger
1   large onion, diced
1   can whole kernel corn, drained
1   large can red kidney beans, drained
1   large can stewed tomatoes
3   cups (drinkable) tomato juice
1   envelope of onion soup mix
3   cups beef broth
1   tsp. ground oregano
1   tsp. ground cumin
$^1/_2$ tsp. ground basil

Using 15 to 19 coals (375°) with bottom heat, brown the sausage and the hamburger with onion. When the meat is well browned, stir in the rest of the ingredients and cook moving coals to a half-and-half ratio, for 25 to 30 minutes. Rotate the oven and lid and stir occasionally while cooking. If needed, add more moisture. Serve hot topped with cheese, diced tomatoes, and sour cream. *Serves 6 to 8.*

Five-Alarm Chili

1½ lbs. ground beef
2 cloves minced garlic
1 large onion, diced
2 large cans chili beans (do not drain)
2 large cans kidney beans
3 4 oz. cans tomato sauce
2 packets of hot chili mix
¾ cup ketchup

2 tsp. cumin
½ tsp. Mexican oregano
2 to 3 Tbsp. chili powder
½ to 1 tsp. ground red pepper
1 to 3 tsp. hot sauce
1 to 2 tsp. salt or to taste
Pepper to taste
1 to 2 cups of water

Brown the ground beef with onion and garlic. Mix in the rest of the ingredients. Cover and cook with 16 to 20 coals (400°), with a 1 (bottom)-to-3 (top) ratio, for 45 minutes to 1 hour. Rotate the oven while cooking and stir occasionally. Add more water or tomato sauce if needed. This dish may be served with cheese and sour cream on top to cut the chili's heat a little. *Serves 8 to 10.*

One-Alarm Chili

Use same ingredients as above, except adjust as follows. Use mild chili mix and decrease seasonings to 1 tsp. cumin, 1 to 2 Tbsp. chili powder. Delete or use very little of the ground red pepper or hot sauce.

Ham & Bean Soup

☞ *Makes use of leftover ham bones or ham hocks.*

Ham bone, ham or ham hocks (no specific amount)
3   carrots, sliced
1   onion, diced
3   stalks of celery, diced
1½ cups dried white beans
Salt and pepper to taste
Water or ham stock (if using left-over ham,
      add any drippings from the roasting pan)

Rinse the beans, then soak them in water overnight. Place the ham or ham hocks in the Dutch oven and cover with water or ham stock. With 16 to 18 coals (350°), with a 4 (bottom)-to-1 (top) ratio, cook for 45 minutes to 1 hour for ham with bones, or 15 to 20 minutes for boneless ham. Remove the ham or ham bones from the stock and run the stock through a mesh strainer to remove any pieces of gristle or bones. When the ham is cool enough to handle, remove the meat from bones and cut it into pieces. Return the stock to the oven, add the beans and ham, then cover and cook for about 45 to 55 minutes more. Add the vegetables and cook until the beans and vegetables are tender. Season with salt and pepper, if needed. *Serves 6 to 8.*

Ham and Broccoli Cheese Soup

☞ *Great served in bread bowls.*

$\frac{1}{2}$ lb. diced ham
1   medium onion, diced
1   large head of broccoli (wash and cut flowerets into large chunks)
2   stalks of celery
3   cups of ham stock or chicken stock
1   lb. process cheese cut into large cubes
2   cups half-and-half or milk
$\frac{1}{2}$ cup flour
Salt and pepper to taste

Place the ham, broccoli, onion, celery, and stock into the Dutch oven, then add just enough water to cover the vegetables if the stock does not cover. Cover and cook using 14 to 16 coals (350°), with half-and-half ratio, until the vegetables are tender, about 15 minutes. While the vegetables are cooking, mix the flour with the half-and-half in a shaker or with a wire whisk until smooth. When the vegetables are done, add the half-and-half mixture. Cook until the flour has cooked and thickened the soup. Add the cheese, then return to heat until the cheese has melted, stirring occasionally. Rotate the oven and lid while cooking and add more liquid, if needed. Season with salt and pepper to taste and serve hot. *Serves 6 to 8.*

Hash Brown Soup

☞ *This is a fast and easy soup that is great served with thick crusty bread.*

2   lbs. frozen shredded hash browns
1   onion diced
2   cups cooked diced chicken
2   cups cooked diced broccoli
1   small brick of processed cheese cut into chunks
3   cups chicken broth
$^1/_2$ cup crisp bacon broken into bits
$1^1/_2$ cups milk
$^1/_2$ cup butter
$^1/_4$ cup of flour
Salt and pepper to taste

Cook the onion in butter until it is tender, then stir in the broth, chicken, potatoes and broccoli. Cover and cook, using 15 to 19 coals (375°), at a 1 (bottom)-to-2 (top) ratio, until the potatoes are tender. When the vegetables are tender, mix the milk and flour together in a shaker-type container and shake until no lumps remain in the flour. Bring the broth to a boil, then stir in milk and flour mixture, bacon and cheese. Cook until the flour cooks and thickens the soup. Season with salt and pepper to taste. *Serves 6 to 8.*

Italian Meat Ball Soup

1   lb. ground beef
½   lb. ground Italian sausage
½   cup bread crumbs
1   beaten egg
1   large onion, diced
2   cloves of minced garlic
1   large jar spaghetti sauce
1   large can whole tomatoes
    (break up tomatoes slightly with spoon)
½   lb. sliced fresh mushrooms
1   tsp. basil
1   tsp. oregano
½   tsp. fennel seed
3   cups cooked macaroni
1 to 2 cups water
Salt and pepper to taste

Mix together the egg, bread crumbs, garlic, onion and ½ of the oregano. Then blend in both meats and knead until mixed well. Shape the meat mixture into small balls. Then, working in batches, cook the meatballs over medium heat in the Dutch oven. When all the meatballs are cooked, stir in the rest of the ingredients. Cover and cook, using 15 to 19 coals (375°), with a 1 (bottom)-to-2 (top) ratio, for 20 to 25 minutes. *Serves 6 to 8.*

Short Rib Stew

☞ *This is an unusual stew that tastes a lot like pot roast.*

1½ lbs. beef short ribs
4   potatoes cut into large cubes
1½ cups sliced carrots
½   cup diced celery
1   large onion, diced
1   cup frozen peas
1   cup kernel corn
1   can kidney beans
4   cups hot beef broth
2   whole bay leaves
Water and flour for thickening broth, if desired
Seasonings: garlic powder, salt, pepper, and seasoning salt to taste

Season the ribs with the above seasonings, then brown them in the Dutch. Cook until the ribs are well browned. Then, stir in the hot beef broth and bay leaves. Cover and cook, using 15 to 19 coals (375°), with a 2 (bottom)-to-3 (top) ratio, for 40 to 45 minutes. Add the potatoes, onion, carrots and celery, then cover and cook until the vegetables are tender. Stir in the rest of the ingredients and cook them for an additional 15 minutes. Remove the bay leaves and thicken the broth with flour and water if desired. *Serves 6 to 8.*

Section Four

Side Dishes

Apple and Squash Bake

2	butternut squash cut into cubes
4	apples, cored and wedged, with or without peels
1	cup apple juice
$^2/_3$	cup raisins
4	Tbsp. brown sugar
1	tsp. cinnamon
$^1/_2$	tsp. nutmeg
$^1/_4$	cup melted butter

Mix all the ingredients in the Dutch oven. Cover and cook with 16 to 20 coals (400°), with a 1 (bottom)-to-3 (top) ratio, for 20 to 25 minutes or until tender. *Serves 6 to 8.*

Broccoli Casserole

2	10-oz. packages of frozen broccoli (cooked and drained)
2	cans cream of chicken soup
1	cup mayonnaise
2	Tbsp. lemon juice
$^1/_2$	tsp. curry powder
Salt and pepper to taste	
2	cups grated cheddar cheese
2	cups buttered bread crumbs

In a large bowl mix together the soup, mayonnaise, lemon juice, cheese, curry and salt and pepper to taste. Gently fold in the broccoli, then pour it into the greased Dutch oven. Sprinkle bread crumbs on top, then cover and cook, using 16 to 19 coals (375°), with a 1 (bottom)-to-2 (top) ratio, for 20 to 25 minutes or until hot and bubbly. *Serves 8 to 10.*

Hot & Spicy Onion Rings

☞ *This batter also can be used to make Onion Blossoms if you have a blossom cutter.*

2   large onions, sliced thick, then separated to form rings
1   egg
1   cup milk
1   cup flour
1   tsp. salt
1   tsp. ground red pepper
$1/4$ tsp. oregano
$1/8$ tsp. cumin
Oil for deep-fat frying

Combine the egg, milk, flour and seasoning and mix until the batter is smooth. Heat about 2 inches of oil in the Dutch oven. This will take about 16 to 20 coals (350° to 375°) at bottom heat only. Dip the onion slices into the batter, then fry them in the hot oil, a few at a time. Turn them over to cook both sides, then remove them with a slotted spoon and drain them on paper towels. Serve with ketchup, ranch dressing or horseradish sauce (recipe is on page 83). *Serves 4 to 6.*

Hot Cocoa Mix

1	2 lb. box of instant chocolate (the Quick kind, made with milk)	1	16 oz. jar of coffee creamer
		1	lb. powdered sugar
		8	oz. powdered milk

Mix everything together thoroughly, then store in an air-tight container. Use 3 to 4 heaping tablespoons of mix to one cup of very hot or boiling water. *Makes 35 to 45 servings.*

Old Fashioned Baked Beans

3	cups dry beans (all pinto or a variety of beans)	1/2	lb. bacon
1	cup molasses	1/2	lb. ground beef
1 1/2	tsp. mustard	1	cup brown sugar
1	large onion, diced	2	8-oz. cans tomato sauce
1	green pepper, diced (optional)		Salt and pepper to taste
			Bottled hot sauce to taste

Rinse and cook the beans according to the package instructions. Fry the bacon and hamburger in the Dutch oven until the bacon is crisp and the hamburger is well browned. Add the onion and green pepper and cook until tender. Add the beans and the rest of the ingredients to the Dutch oven and stir to mix well. Bake with 16 to 20 coals (400°), with 1 (top)-to-3 (bottom) ratio, for 1 hour. Stir occasionally, and rotate the oven and lid while cooking. *Serves 12 people as a main course, or 25 as a side dish.*

Fried Apples

☞ *Great with baked ham or barbecue ribs.*

6   tart apples (cored and sliced thick, or wedged;
       do not peel)
½ to 1 cup water
¾ to 1 cup sugar
½   cup butter
Cinnamon and nutmeg to taste
½   tsp. salt

Mix all the ingredients in the Dutch oven. Cover and cook with 14 to 15 coals (350°), with a half-and-half ratio, for 15 to 20 minutes or until the apples are soft. Add more water as needed, and stir occasionally. When the apples are tender, adjust the seasoning and serve hot. *Serves 6.*

Homemade Root Beer

5   gallons of water
3   oz. root beer extract
9   cups of sugar
5   lbs. dry ice

Combine the water and extract in a large water jug with a spout on the bottom, or something similar. Stir in the sugar until it has dissolved, then add the ice and mix it again. Let this sit for a few minutes to start the carbonation process, then stir again and enjoy. Makes 5 gallons of root beer..

Safety Note: Use great caution when using dry ice. Never touch it with bare skin. Always wear gloves, or hold it in the paper it comes wrapped in. Do not store dry ice in your freezer.

Honey and Spice Carrots

1 lb. package of peeled baby carrots
½ cup chicken broth
¼ cup butter
¼ cup honey
½ tsp. salt
½ tsp. nutmeg

Place everything in the Dutch oven and toss to mix it. Cover and cook with 16 to 20 coals (400°), with 1 (bottom)-to-3 (top) ratio, for 20 to 30 minutes or until the carrots are tender. Stir occasionally and add more broth or butter if needed. *Serves 6 to 8.*

Hoppin' John

1   large onion, sliced
1½ cups black-eyed peas
2   cloves minced garlic
1   green pepper, diced
¼   tsp. red pepper
½   tsp. black pepper
½ to 1 tsp. salt or to taste
1   bay leaf
8   oz. bacon cut into one-inch pieces
2   cups hot cooked rice
Hot sauce

Rinse the black-eyed peas, then soak them in water overnight. Using 17 to 23 coals (425°), with bottom heat only, bring the peas and about 5 to 6 cups of water to boil in the Dutch oven. Add the onion, green pepper, garlic, and seasonings, then cover and cook moving coals to 4 (bottom)-to-1 (top) ratio, for about 1 hour. Stir occasionally and add more water if needed. While the peas are cooking, fry the bacon in a frying pan, then add it to the Dutch oven along with any drippings that are in the frying pan. Cook for an additional 35 to 45 minutes or until the peas are very soft. Stir often, add more water if needed. When the peas are soft, discard the bay leaf, then remove about half of the peas and mash them with a potato masher. (Try to remove and mash only the peas, not the vegetables or bacon.) Return the mashed peas to the stockpot and add additional salt or pepper, if needed. Serve hot over rice, with hot sauce. *Serves 6 to 8.*

Hush Puppies

☞ *Easy to make and very filling. Leftover meat, diced green peppers, canned green chilies or kernels of corn may be added.*

1½ cups cornmeal
¼   cup flour
1   Tbsp. baking powder
¾   tsp. salt
2   eggs
¾   cup buttermilk
¼   cup diced onion
Oil for frying

Blend the dry ingredients together, then stir in the eggs and buttermilk until well blended. Add the onion and mix well. Using bottom heat only, heat about 2 to 3 inches of oil in the Dutch oven with 14 to 15 coals until it reaches between 325 and 375 degrees. (Use a thermometer when deep-frying; if the oil is too cold, the food will be greasy; if it is too hot the oil may ignite. Gently lower the food into the hot oil; if food is dropped, oil can splash and cause burns.) To cook Hush Puppies, either roll the batter into balls or lower it by the spoonful into the hot oil. Turn over to cook both sides until golden brown, about 3 to 5 minutes. Serve hot. *Serves 4 to 8.*

Southern Corn Casserole

$^1/_3$ cup diced green pepper
$^1/_3$ cup diced onion
$^1/_4$ cup flour
3   Tbsp. butter
1   can cream corn
$^1/_2$ tsp. salt
Pepper to taste
2   cans whole kernel corn
2   cans sliced mushrooms
1   cup grated cheddar cheese
$1^1/_2$ cups buttered bread crumbs

Cook the onion and pepper in butter until tender. Stir in the flour and mix until the flour has absorbed the butter. Add the cream corn and cook until the mixture has thickened. Mix in the salt and pepper, kernel corn, mushrooms and cheese, then top with bread crumbs. Cook with 16 to 20 coals (400°), with a 1 (bottom)-to-3 (top) ratio, for 20 to 25 minutes. *Serves 6 to 8.*

Section Five

Breads

Buttermilk Biscuits

2   cups flour
4   tsp. baking powder
$^{1}/_{2}$ tsp. salt
$^{2}/_{3}$ cup shortening
$^{1}/_{2}$ to $^{3}/_{4}$ cup buttermilk

In a large bowl combine the flour, baking powder, and salt. Cut in the shortening until the mixture is crumbly, then stir in the buttermilk until the mixture is moist. (Often the full $^{3}/_{4}$ cup of buttermilk will not be needed.) Turn out the biscuits onto a floured surface and roll the dough to a $^{3}/_{4}$-inch thickness. Cut the dough with a biscuit cutter and bake with 17 to 22 coals (425°), with 1 (bottom)-to-3 (top) ratio, for 10 to 15 minutes or until golden brown. Rotate the lid and oven while cooking. *Serves 6 to 8.*

Cheesy Spoon Bread with Corn

1   onion, diced
$^{1}/_{4}$ cup butter
2   beaten eggs
1   can cream corn
$^{1}/_{4}$ tsp. salt
$^{1}/_{4}$ tsp. pepper

$1^{1}/_{2}$ cups sour cream
1   8$^{1}/_{2}$-oz. corn bread mix
1   diced jalapeno pepper
2   cups grated
     cheddar cheese

Saute the onion and Jalapeno pepper with butter in the Dutch oven until tender. In a bowl, mix together the eggs, sour cream, both cans of corn, salt and pepper. Stir in the corn bread mix and gently mix until just blended. Add the cooked onion and jalapeno and mix again, then mix in 1½ cups of the cheese. Pour into an oiled Dutch oven, then top with the rest of the cheese. Cover and cook with 16 to 19 coals (375°), with a 1 (bottom)-to-3 (top) ratio, for 35 to 45 minutes, or until a toothpick inserted into the bread comes out clean. Serve hot. *Serves 6 to 8.*

Cowboy Cheese Bread

2½	cups flour	2	Tbsp. dried parsley
2	eggs	¼	tsp. garlic powder
½	cup milk	1	Tbsp. sugar
¼	cup butter-flavored shortening	½	cup melted butter, divided in half
¾	tsp. salt	1	cup grated cheddar cheese
2	tsp. baking powder		
1½	tsp. dried onion	¼	cup Parmesan cheese

Mix all dry ingredients and seasonings together. Do not mix in either cheese at this time. Cut the shortening and ¼ cup of the butter into the dry ingredients; mix until it resembles a coarse meal. Mix the eggs and milk together; then add to the flour mixture and mix again. Add both cheeses, and kneed until the cheese is worked through. Roll the dough out into 12-inch circle, then cut it with a pizza cutter into pie-shaped wedges. Place the wedges the way they were cut into an oiled Dutch oven, then drizzle with the remaining butter. Cover and cook with 16 to 22 coals (400°), with 1 (bottom)-to-3 (top) ratio, for 20 to 30 minutes or until no longer doughy inside. *Serves 8 to 10.*

Dutch Oven Corn Bread

☞ *This recipe was designed for a 14-inch Dutch oven but can be cooked in a 12-inch oven by increasing the cooking time 8 to 10 minutes or by scooping out 1½ cups of the batter.*

2   cups cornmeal
2   cups flour
1   pudding-in-the-mix yellow cake mix,
     prepared as directed on package
1   tsp. salt
2½   Tbsp. baking powder
2   cups milk
2   eggs
⅔   cup oil

Mix together the cornmeal, flour, salt and baking powder, then mix in the eggs, milk, and the oil. Combine the cake batter and cornmeal mixture, then pour into a well-oiled 14- or 12-inch Dutch oven. Cover and cook with 17 to 22 coals (425°), with a 1 (bottom)-to-3 (top) ratio, for 35 to 45 minutes. Rotate the oven and lid while cooking and check occasionally. *Serves 8 to 12.*

Easy Herb Biscuits

3   cups biscuit mix
$^1/_2$ tsp. fennel seed
$^1/_4$ tsp. garlic powder
1   Tbsp. sugar
1   tsp. dried basil leaves
1   Tbsp. dried onion
$^1/_2$ cup melted butter (do not use margarine)
Milk

Mix the herbs and seasonings with the biscuit mix, then add enough milk to make a manageable dough. Roll out the dough and cut it with a biscuit cutter, or into strips. Pour half of the melted butter into the bottom of the Dutch oven, then place the biscuits on top. Pour the remaining butter on top and cook with 15 to 19 coals (375°), at a 1 (bottom)-to-3 (top) ratio, for 18 to 25 minutes or until biscuits are cooked through. Rotate the lid and oven while cooking. *Serves 6.*

Herbed Bread

3$^1/_2$ to 4 cups flour
1$^1/_2$ cups warm water
1   tsp. salt
$^1/_4$ cup sugar
$^1/_4$ cup oil
1   tsp. fennel seed
1   tsp. dried basil leaves
1   clove minced garlic

Mix the warm water with the yeast and sugar, then add the oil and seasonings and 3$^1/_2$ cups of the flour and knead the dough until smooth, using additional flour if the dough is sticky. Let the dough sit for 20 minutes then form into a round, flat loaf. Brush the loaf with oil and place it in a generously oiled Dutch oven. Cover and cook with 16 to 20 coals (400°), with a 1 (bottom)-to-3 (top) ratio, for approximately 45 to 55 minutes. Rotate the oven and lid while cooking and check occasionally. This bread is best served hot from the oven or toasted. *Serves 6.*

Italian Garlic Bread

Bread:

2½ cups flour
1 cup warm water
1 tsp. salt
1 Tbsp. sugar
½ tsp. garlic powder
1 tsp. Italian seasoning
1 package quick-rise yeast
¼ cup olive oil

Topping:

2 Tbsp. melted butter
Garlic powder
½ cup Parmesan cheese
1 cup grated mozzarella cheese

Mix the yeast and sugar into warm water and let the mixture sit until the yeast is dissolved. Add salt, oil, and seasonings to the yeast mixture, then stir in flour a little at a time. Knead until smooth. Roll out the dough and place it into the bottom of an oiled Dutch oven. For topping, mix the melted butter, garlic powder and Parmesan cheese together, then brush over the top of the dough. Then sprinkle with mozzarella, cover, and cook with 16 to 19 coals (375°) for 18 to 22 minutes. *Serves 6 to 8.*

Pizza Crust

☞ *Makes a deep-dish pizza that is out of this world.*

1   Tbsp. yeast or one yeast packet
1   cup warm water
1   Tbsp. sugar
¹/₄ to ¹/₂ cup olive oil or cooking oil
1   tsp. salt
3   cups flour

Mix the yeast with water and sugar, then let it sit for 5 minutes. Stir in the oil and salt, then add the flour and knead until smooth, adding more flour if needed. Let the dough rest for 10 to 15 minutes. Roll the dough into a 13- to 14-inch circle; then place it in the bottom of a well-oiled Dutch oven. Curve the dough up the sides to create a shallow bowl for toppings. Top as desired, then cover and cook with 17 to 18 coals (375°), with a 1 (bottom)-to-3 (top) ratio, for 20 to 30 minutes.

☞ *Tip for making great pizza:* Cook the mushrooms, green peppers and onions before placing them on an uncooked pizza crust to prevent extra moisture from accumulating while cooking and prevent the crust from becoming soggy.

☞ *Herb Crust:* To add a little zip to pizza, try adding herbs to the crust. Before adding flour, add 2 Tbsp. Parmesan cheese, ¹/₂ tsp. fennel seeds, ¹/₂ tsp. basil or oregano leaves, and ¹/₄ tsp. garlic powder. Bread sticks can be made out of this recipe. Brush them with melted butter after cooking. *Serves 4 to 6.*

Section Six

Main Dishes

Barbecue Chicken Pizza

1   recipe pizza crust
1   cup spicy barbecue sauce
2 to 3 cups grated mozzarella cheese
$\frac{1}{2}$ onion, sliced thin
$\frac{1}{2}$ green pepper, sliced thin
1   tomato, sliced thin
1 to 2 cups cooked shredded chicken

Oil the Dutch oven. Roll out the pizza crust and place it in the oven as directed in the Pizza Crust recipe (page 76). Pour barbecue sauce over the crust and spread evenly. Top with chicken, cheese, and vegetables. Place sliced tomatoes on the top. Cover and cook with 17 to 18 coals (375°), with a 1 (bottom)-to-3 (top) ratio, for 30 to 35 minutes or until the dough is cooked through. Rotate the lid and oven, and check pizza occasionally while cooking. *Serves 4 to 6.*

Beef Barbecue Sandwich

2   lbs. of beef pot roast
1   bottle liquid smoke
1   can cola soda or beef broth
1 to 2 bottles barbecue sauce
Swiss or cheddar cheese slices
Sauteed onions
Toasted onion rolls or hoagie buns

Marinate the pot roast in liquid smoke overnight. Place the roast in an oiled Dutch oven and pour the soda over the top. Cover and cook with 16 to 20 coals (400°), with 1 (bottom)-to-3 (top) ratio, for $1\frac{1}{2}$ to 2 hours or until the meat separates easily. Add more moisture if needed, and rotate the oven and lid while cooking. Using a fork, shred the meat, then stir in the barbecue sauce and heat through. Serve on hot toasted buns with cheese and onions. *Serves 6 to 8.*

Barbecue Chicken Deluxe

6   boneless, skinless chicken breasts
1/4 cup vegetable oil
4   Tbsp. liquid smoke
1   Tbsp. hot sauce

Mix the oil, liquid smoke, and hot sauce together, then marinate the chicken in a refrigerator in the mixture for at least 2 hours (overnight is best). Turn the chicken occasionally to insure even marinating. Brown the chicken with a little oil in the Dutch oven, using medium bottom heat with 15 to 19 coals (375°). Turn the chicken to brown both sides. When the chicken is browned, proceed as directed below.

1   cup barbecue sauce
12   slices of cooked bacon
1 to 2 cups of grated cheddar or Monterey Jack cheese

Pour the barbecue sauce over the chicken, then place 2 slices of bacon on each chicken breast. Top with grated cheese. Cover and cook, with 1 (bottom)-to-3 (top) ratio, for 10 to 15 minutes or until the cheese melts and the sauce is hot. *Serves 6.*

Broccoli and Cheese Rice with Chicken

4 to 6 boneless, skinless chicken breasts, cut into chunks
2   packages of fast-cook broccoli and cheese rice mix
Hot water and butter as directed on the rice-mix package
3   cups broccoli flowerets
3   cups grated cheddar cheese
$^1/_2$ cup additional butter
$^1/_2$ tsp. curry powder
Salt and pepper to taste

Brown the chicken in a small amount of oil or butter, until cooked through. Reserve half of the cheese, then stir in the rest of the ingredients. Cover and cook with 17 to 22 coals (425°), at a 1 (bottom)-to-2 (top) ratio, for 25 to 35 minutes or until the rice is tender. Stir occasionally; add more water if needed. When the rice is done, top with the remaining cheese, then cover and cook until the cheese melts. *Serves 5 to 7.*

Cabbage Rolls

2   lbs. ground beef
1   cup milk
1   cup bread crumbs
$^3/_4$ cup finely diced onion
$^3/_4$ cup uncooked rice
1   tsp. salt
$^1/_2$ tsp. pepper
$^1/_2$ tsp. nutmeg
1   large head of cabbage
Salted water to boil cabbage leaves
1 to 2 quarts tomato juice (drinkable tomato juice,
       not tomato sauce)

Mix everything except the cabbage and tomato juice together in a large bowl, then let the mixture sit for 15 minutes. While the meat mixture sits, remove the core of the cabbage and place the leaves in boiling salted water until softened. Do not overcook. Drain the leaves and allow them to cool slightly. Mix the meat mixture again and shape it into small loaves (a handful, almost baseball-size, works well). Roll a cabbage leaf around the meat loaf, tucking the ends under to enclose all the meat. (Roll the smaller leaves inside the larger leaves along with the meat, to avoid wasting leaves that are too small to use.) Tie them with string, thread, or pin them with a toothpick to seal. Place the cabbage rolls in the Dutch oven, then pour tomato juice over the top. Add water, if needed, to cover the rolls. Bake with 17 to 22 coals (425°), with 1 (bottom)-to-3 (top) ratio, for 1 to 1$^1/_2$ hours until the meat is done. Rotate the oven and lid while cooking, and add more juice if needed. *Serves 6 to 8.*

Cajun Catfish
with Horseradish Sauce

☞ *These spicy filets are great for people who like to add a little heat in their food.*

Catfish

3 to 4 catfish filets
1   cup flour
$^1/_2$ cup bread crumbs
1   egg beaten with
     3 Tbsp. milk

$^1/_4$ to $^1/_2$ tsp. ground red pepper
$^1/_4$ to $^1/_2$ tsp. Cajun seasoning
$^1/_2$ tsp. salt
Oil for frying

Mix the flour, bread crumbs, and seasoning together on a plate or other type of flat surface. Heat the Dutch oven with about $^1/_2$ inch of oil in the bottom, using 15 to 20 coals (375°). Dip the catfish filets into the egg-and-milk mixture, then into the crumb mixture, turning to coat both sides. Then fry in hot oil, turning to cook both sides until fish flakes easily. Serve with sauce below. *Serves 3 to 4.*

Horseradish Sauce

$^3/_4$ cup mayonnaise
2   Tbsp. ketchup
2   tsp. cream style
     horseradish

$^1/_4$ tsp. salt
$^1/_4$ tsp. oregano
$^1/_4$ tsp. paprika
$^1/_4$ tsp. ground red pepper

Mix everything together until it is well blended. For a more intense flavor, let sit 24 hours before using.

Chicken and Dumplings

Chicken

    5 to 6 lb. stewing chicken, or 2 smaller fryers
    5   stalks celery, finely diced
    2   carrots, thinly sliced
    1   onion, diced
    1   bay leaf
    1   tsp. salt
    $1/2$ tsp. pepper
    2   Tbsp. chicken bouillon

Cut the chicken into pieces; remove the skin if desired. Season the chicken with salt and pepper and place it in the Dutch oven. Add bay leaf, bouillon and onion. Pour enough warm water over the chicken to cover it, then place the lid on the oven. Place 18 to 23 coals (425°), with a half-and-half ratio, and cook for 1 to $1^{1}/_{2}$ hours. Add celery and carrots, and cook until the vegetables are tender. While the chicken is cooking, prepare the dumplings (recipe follows).

Dumplings

    2   cups flour
    4   tsp. baking powder
    1   tsp. salt
    1   cup milk
    $1/4$ cup melted butter

Mix all the ingredients together and stir until moistened. Two tablespoons of parsley or snipped chives may be added for a little color. When the chicken and the vegetables are done, bring the broth to a boil and drop the dumplings by table-spoonsful into the broth and chicken. Cover tightly with the lid, then change the heat to 1 (bottom)-to-3 (top) ratio, and cook for 15 to 20 minutes. *Do not lift cover* for the first 15 minutes. When the dumplings are done, remove the chicken and dumplings and arrange them on a platter. Heat the leftover stock and vegetables to a boil. If less than 2 to 3 cups of broth remains, add additional water or chicken to the broth. Thicken the stock with water and flour mixed together, and season with additional salt and pepper, if necessary. To serve, spoon the broth and vegetables over the chicken and dumplings on the platter. *Serves 8 to 10.*

Chicken Enchilada Casserole

2   cups cooked chicken
2   small cans of diced green chilies (do not drain)
1   carton of sour cream
2   cans cream of chicken soup
8 to 10 large flour tortillas (corn tortillas may be used, if preferred)
2   cups grated Colby Jack cheese

Mix the sour cream, soup, and green chilies (with juice) together. Spread a layer of this sour-cream mixture on the bottom of the Dutch oven. Layer about 3 tortillas over the top of this, cutting the tortillas as needed to cover the entire mixture. Layer half of the chicken, then about $^1/_3$ of the cheese over this, then spoon some of the sauce onto the top. Cover with another layer of 3 tortillas, then the other half of chicken, $^1/_3$ of the cheese, and more sauce. Use 3 more tortillas, then cover with the rest of the sauce and the rest of the cheese. Cover and cook with 16 to 20 coals (400°) with 1 (bottom)-to-3 (top) ratio, for 25 to 30 minutes. Rotate the oven and lid while cooking. *Serves 6 to 8.*

Chicken Parmesan

6 boneless, skinless chicken breasts
1 egg
3 Tbsp. milk
1 1/2 cups dry bread crumbs seasoned with:
  1/2 tsp. salt
  1/2 tsp. garlic powder
  1/2 tsp. ground oregano
  1/2 tsp. ground basil
  1/4 cup Parmesan cheese
6 thick slices mozzarella cheese
2 to 3 cups spaghetti sauce
Butter or oil for frying

Using 16 to 20 coals (400°), heat the oil or butter, using bottom heat only. Beat the egg and milk together until frothy, then dip the chicken in the egg mixture. Coat it with the bread crumbs and the seasoning mixture. Fry in hot oil or butter, turning the chicken to brown both sides. Cook until the chicken is no longer pink inside. When the chicken is done, pour spaghetti sauce over the top, then top with cheese. Cover and cook, moving coals to a 1 (bottom)-to-3 (top) ratio for about 10 minutes, or until the cheese is melted and the sauce is hot. This can be served over hot spaghetti noodles with additional sauce, if desired. *Serves 6.*

Chile Relleno Casserole

$^1\!/_2$ lb. bulk spicy pork sausage
$^1\!/_2$ lb. ground beef
1   onion, diced
1   cup milk
$^1\!/_2$ tsp. salt
6   eggs
$^1\!/_2$ cup flour
3   7-oz. cans whole green chilies, seeded
1   cup grated cheddar cheese
2   cups grated Monterey Jack cheese

Brown the ground beef, sausage, and onion in the Dutch oven using 12 to 15 coals with bottom heat only; remove it from the oven when browned. Beat together milk, eggs, salt and flour, then stir in one cup of the Monterey Jack cheese and all of the cheddar cheese. Place a layer of green chilies on the bottom of the oiled Dutch oven, then sprinkle half of the meat mixture over the chilies. Pour half of the egg-and-cheese mixture over this; then add another layer of chilies. Top with the remaining meat, egg mixture, and the last cup of cheese. Cover and cook with 16 to 22 coals (425°) with a 1 (bottom)-to-3 (top) ratio, for 30 to 40 minutes. Rotate the oven and lid while cooking. *Serves 6 to 8.*

Curried Turkey with Rice

2   turkey breasts cut into chunks
2   packages of fast-cooking chicken-flavored rice mix
Hot water and butter as directed on the rice-mix package
$^1/_4$ cup peanut butter
1 to 2 tsp. curry
$^1/_2$ tsp. ginger
$^1/_2$ tsp.cinnamon
$^3/_4$ cup raisins (optional)

Using 12 to 15 coals with bottom heat only, cook the turkey in a small amount of oil or butter until it is no longer pink inside. Add the rest of the ingredients to the oven, then stir to mix well. Cover and cook with 17 to 22 coals (425°), with a 1 (bottom)-to-2 (top) ratio, for 25 to 35 minutes. Stir occasionally and add more water if needed. *Serves 6 to 8.*

Corned Beef Dinner

3 to 4 lbs. beef brisket
1   chopped onion
2   cloves minced garlic
3   bay leaves
Salt and pepper to taste
6   medium-size potatoes, cut in wedges
6   carrots, peeled and cut into large chunks
1   small head of cabbage, cut into wedges

Place the brisket in the Dutch oven, then pour enough hot water over the brisket to cover it. Add the chopped onion, garlic, bay leaves, salt and pepper. Cover and simmer with 18 to 23 coals (425°), with 3 (bottom)-to-1 (top) ratio, for 2 to 3 hours. Rotate the oven occasionally while cooking and add more liquid if needed. When the meat is very tender, add the carrots and potatoes and cook them until the vegetables are starting to soften. Add the cabbage wedges and cook 15 to 20 minutes longer, until all vegetables are tender. *Serves 6 to 8.*

Fast and Easy Lasagna

1^1/$_2$ lbs. ground beef
2   cloves minced garlic
1   onion, diced
1   large jar of spaghetti sauce
1   pint Ricotta cheese
2 to 3 cups grated Mozzarella cheese
^{1}/$_2$ to ^{3}/$_4$ cup Parmesan cheese
1   box lasagna noodles, cooked

Brown the hamburger with garlic and onion in the Dutch oven. Remove it from the oven when done. Spoon some of the spaghetti sauce into the bottom of the Dutch oven, then place a layer of noodles, followed by meat, Parmesan and Mozzarella cheeses, and more sauce. Cover this layer with noodles, then a layer of Ricotta cheese and another layer of noodles, then repeat with another layer of meat, cheeses, sauce and the remaining noodles. Finish off with the rest of the sauce and Parmesan and Mozzarella cheese. Cover and cook with 16 to 20 coals (400°) with 1 (bottom)-to-3 (top) ratio, for 20 to 25 minutes. Rotate the oven and lid while cooking. *Serves 6 to 8.*

Ginger & Orange Steak

2 to 3 lbs. steak of your choice
1   small can of orange juice
$^1/_2$ cup brown sugar
$^1/_2$ cup beef broth
$^1/_4$ to $^1/_2$ tsp. grated fresh ginger (do not use dried or ground)
Salt and pepper to taste
Oil for cooking steak

The steak can be cut into wide strips and fried, or left whole. Brown the steak in a small amount of oil in the Dutch oven using 16 to 20 coals (400°), and bottom heat only. Mix the rest of the ingredients in a bowl, then pour them over the steak. Cover and cook, moving the coals to a half-and-half ratio, for 20 to 25 minutes. *Serves 6 to 8.*

Grandma's Pot Roast

3 to 4 lbs. beef chuck roast
1   bay leaf
2   cloves garlic, minced
1   cup hot water
2   medium onions, cut into wedges
8   potatoes, cut into wedges
6   carrots, cut into 2-inch pieces
2   stalks of celery, cut into large pieces
Salt and pepper to taste

Rub the outside of the roast with garlic, then season it with salt and pepper. Brown the roast in the Dutch oven with a small amount of oil; cook until the roast is well browned. Add the water and the bay leaf to the Dutch oven. Cover and roast with 17 to 22 coals (425°), with a half-and-half ratio, for 35 to 40 minutes, adding more water if necessary. Place the onions, potatoes, celery, and carrots around the roast. Season the vegetables with salt and pepper, then cover and cook for an additional 40 to 45 minutes. Drain the drippings from the meat and thicken with flour and water to make gravy. *Serves 6 to 8.*

Honey Lime Ribs

3 to 4 lbs. beef short ribs
1   small onion, diced
2   cloves minced garlic
1   can lemon-lime soda
$^1/_2$ cup honey
4   Tbsp. Dijon mustard
$^1/_2$ cup sweetened, bottled lime juice
2   tsp. liquid smoke
4   Tbsp. brown sugar
$^1/_2$ cup melted butter
Salt to taste

Brown the ribs in the Dutch oven with a small amount of oil until well browned. Mix the other ingredients in a bowl, then pour them over the top of the ribs. Cover and cook with 17 to 22 coals (425°), with 1 (bottom)-to-3 (top) ratio, for 45 to 55 minutes or until the ribs are tender. Rotate the oven and lid while cooking, and add moisture if needed. *Serves 3 to 4 with bone-in ribs and 6 to 8 with boneless ribs.*

Honey Orange Chicken

6   boneless, skinless chicken breasts, cut into chunks
2   eggs beaten with 2 Tbsp. milk
Cornstarch
Oil for frying
1   6-oz can frozen orange juice
1/4   cup honey
1/4   cup brown sugar
2   Tbsp. cider vinegar
2   Tbsp. dried onion
1/4   tsp. garlic powder
Salt and pepper to taste
Hot cooked rice

Heat about 1/2 inch of oil in the Dutch oven using 15 to 19 coals, heating oil to 350-375 degrees. Roll the chicken pieces in cornstarch, then dip them in the eggs and fry in hot oil; turn them to cook both sides until the chicken is cooked through. Cook in batches, removing the cooked pieces from the oven; repeat until all chicken is cooked. Mix together orange juice, honey, and the rest of the ingredients, except the rice. Return all the chicken pieces to the oven, then cover them with sauce. Cover and cook with 16 to 20 coals (400°), with 1 (bottom)-to-3 (top) ratio, for 10 to 15 minutes. Serve hot over rice. *Serves 6 to 8.*

Italian Style Pizza

1   recipe pizza crust
3   Roma tomatoes, chopped
1   clove minced garlic
$^1/_2$ tsp. salt
2   Tbsp. each of fresh basil and oregano,
    or 2 tsp. dried basil and oregano leaves
1   small jar of oil-marinated artichoke hearts,
    chopped (drain and reserve liquid)
1   small package sliced pepperoni
1   small package sliced salami (about 5 oz.)
$^2/_3$ cup sliced olives
$^1/_2$ red onion, sliced thin
$^1/_2$ bell pepper, sliced thin
$^1/_2$ cup Parmesan cheese
2 to 3 cups Mozzarella cheese

Oil the Dutch oven, then line the bottom with pizza crust. Mix liquid from the artichoke hearts (no more than $^1/_4$ cup) with the tomatoes, clove of garlic, salt, basil and oregano, then spread the mixture on the pizza crust. Top with meats, cheeses, then vegetables. Cover and cook with 17 to 18 coals (400°), with a 1 (bottom)-to-3 (top) ratio, for 30 to 40 minutes. Rotate the oven and lid while cooking, and check the pizza occasionally. *Serves 4 to 6.*

☞ *Tip for making great pizza:* Cook the mushrooms, green peppers and onions before placing them on an uncooked pizza crust to prevent extra moisture from accumulating while cooking and prevent the crust from becoming soggy.

Lemon & Dill Cod

1 to 2 lbs. cod filets (cut into serving-size pieces)
1 cube of butter
1 Tbsp. fresh dill, or 1 tsp. dried dill
$\frac{1}{2}$ cup diced onion
1   clove minced garlic
2   Tbsp. lemon juice

In a sauce pan saute the onion and garlic in butter until tender, then mix in the lemon juice and dill and saute for 2 minutes more. Place the fish filets in an oiled Dutch oven, then pour the butter sauce over the top. Cover and cook with 16 to 20 coals (375°), with a 1 (bottom)-to-2 (top) ratio, for 20 to 25 minutes or until the fish flakes easily. Serve with sauce spooned over the top of the fish. *Serves 4 to 8.*

Meat Lovers' Pizza

1   recipe pizza crust
$^1/_2$ lb. bulk sausage, browned
$^1/_2$ lb. hamburger, browned
1   small package sliced pepperoni
$^1/_2$ onion, sliced thin
$^1/_2$ green pepper, sliced thin
1   small can sliced olives
1   tomato, sliced thin
2 to 3 cups Mozzarella cheese
Parmesan cheese to taste
$^1/_2$ to 1 small jar of spaghetti sauce

Add to spaghetti sauce:
$^1/_4$ tsp. cinnamon
$^1/_4$ tsp. ground red pepper
$^1/_4$ tsp. ground basil

Oil the Dutch oven, then line the bottom with crust. Top with spaghetti sauce and meats, then cheeses and vegetables, ending with sliced tomato. Cover and cook with 17 to 18 coals (400°), with a 1 (bottom)-to-3 (top) ratio, for 30 to 40 minutes. Rotate the oven and lid while cooking, and check the pizza often. *Serves 4 to 6.*

Meatloaf Dinner

Meatloaf

1½ lbs. ground beef
1   egg
1   cup bread crumbs
2   Tbsp. Worcestershire sauce
2   Tbsp. ketchup
1   onion, diced
1   clove minced garlic
½   tsp. salt
1   tsp. mustard

Mix the above ingredients together and form them into a ring in the bottom of the Dutch oven. Cook with 18 to 23 coals, with a 1 (bottom)-to-3 (top) ratio, for 30 to 35 minutes, then add vegetables listed below and top with sauce.

Vegetables

8   sliced potatoes
2   cups sliced or baby carrots
1   onion, sliced
3   stalks of celery, sliced
½   cup hot beef broth
Salt and pepper

Sauce

1   8-oz. can tomato sauce
3   Tbsp. ketchup
1   Tbsp. mustard
3   Tbsp. brown sugar

Place the vegetables around and inside the meatloaf ring. Pour the beef broth over the vegetables, then season with salt and pepper. Mix the sauce ingredients together, then pour it over the meat loaf. Cover and cook for an additional 35 to 45 minutes, or until the meatloaf is done. Rotate the oven and lid while cooking, and add more broth if needed. *Serves 6 to 8.*

New Potatoes with Peas and Pork

$1^1/_2$ lbs. boneless pork, ribs cut into chunks
8 to 10 new potatoes, cut into wedges
$^1/_2$ onion, diced fine
3   cups frozen peas
2   cans cream of mushroom soup mixed with
      1 can of water
$^1/_2$ to 1 tsp. salt
Seasonings: salt, pepper, seasoned salt, and garlic powder

Brown the pork with seasonings in a little oil using 16 to 20 coals, until browned. Stir in the potatoes, onions, mushroom-soup mixture and salt. Cover and cook with 17 to 22 coals (425°), with 1 (bottom)-to-3 (top) ratio, for 25 to 30 minutes. Stir occasionally, adding more water if needed. Stir in the peas and cook for 10 minutes more or until peas and potatoes are tender. *Serves 6 to 8.*

Paradise Island Pork

2   lbs. boneless pork ribs, cut into large chunks
1   small onion, diced fine
1   green pepper, cut into chunks
1   small can of pineapple chunks (do not drain juice)
1/2   cup brown sugar
1/4   cup chili sauce
3   Tbsp. vinegar
2   Tbsp. lime juice
1/4 to 1/2 tsp. ground red pepper
1/2 tsp. each of salt, allspice, and ground ginger
Cornstarch mixed with water (for thickening)
Hot cooked rice

Brown the pork in the Dutch oven over medium heat, adding oil if necessary. When the meat is browned, stir in everything except the rice and cornstarch mixture. Cover and cook with 16 to 20 coals (400°), with a half-and-half ratio, for 25 to 35 minutes. Thicken the sauce with cornstarch, if needed, and serve hot over rice. *Serves 6 to 8.*

Salmon with Lemon and Garlic Butter

☞ *This is a wonderful way to enjoy salmon.*

4   salmon filets
1   cube butter (must be real butter)
$1/2$ cup fresh lemon juice or $1/4$-cup concentrate
1   clove minced garlic
Salt and lemon pepper to taste

Cook the garlic in butter, using 15 to 19 coals (375°) over bottom heat only. When the garlic is tender, add the lemon juice to the butter and whisk until it is slightly blended. Cook the filets in the butter and lemon, turning them to cook both sides. Cook them just until the fish flakes easily. To serve, spoon butter sauce over the fish filets. *Serves 4.*

Seven Layer Dinner

1½ lbs. ground beef
8   potatoes, sliced (with or without peels)
1   large onion, sliced
½   lb. cooked bacon (crumbled)
2   cans chili beans (not drained)
2   cans whole kernel corn (drained)
2   cans tomato soup mixed with 1 can of water
2   cups grated cheese
Garlic powder, salt and pepper to taste

Press the ground beef into the bottom of the Dutch oven, then layer the rest of the ingredients (except the cheese and soup) as they are listed. Season with salt, pepper, and garlic powder after each layer (except the bacon). Pour the soup over the top, then cook with 17 to 23 coals (425°), with a 1 (bottom)-to-2 (top) ratio, for 40 to 50 minutes. Do not stir while cooking. Rotate the lid and oven while cooking, and add more moisture if needed. When done, top with cheese, then cover until the cheese melts. *Serves 6 to 8.*

South of the Border Goulash

1½ lbs. ground beef
1   onion, diced
2   16-oz. cans whole tomatoes
2   packets of taco seasoning
1   can whole-kernel corn
8   oz. dry egg noodles
1½ cups water
Grated cheese
Sour cream

Brown the ground beef with onion using 16 to 20 coals, then stir in everything except the cheese and sour cream. Chop the whole tomatoes slightly with a spoon. Cover and cook with 17 to 22 coals (425°), with a 1 (bottom)-to-2 (top) ratio, for 25 to 30 minutes or until the noodles are tender. Stir occasionally, and add more water if needed. Top with grated cheese, then cover and cook until the cheese has melted. Serve with sour cream. *Serves 6 to 8.*

Spicy Chinese Beef

2   lbs. sirloin steak, cut into large chunks
1   clove minced garlic
$1/2$ cup soy sauce
1   cup beef broth
$1^1/2$ Tbsp. sugar
1   tsp. hot sauce
$1^1/2$ tsp. fresh grated ginger (must be fresh,
      not dried and ground)
1   onion, cut into wedges
1   green pepper, cut into large chunks
3   Tbsp. cornstarch, mixed
      with about $1/2$ cup of water, to thicken the sauce
Cooked rice or oriental noodles

Brown the beef in the Dutch oven with oil, using 17 to 22 coals (425°), with heat on the bottom only, until very well browned. Add the garlic, broth, soy sauce, sugar, hot sauce and ginger. Cover and cook, moving the coals to a half-and-half ratio, until the beef is very tender, about 20 to 25 minutes. Add more broth if needed and stir occasionally during cooking. When the beef is tender, add the onion and pepper, and cook until the vegetables are crisp-tender. Thicken with cornstarch mixture, and serve over noodles or rice. *Serves 6 to 8.*

Spicy Pasta Stir Fry

☞ *Dutch oven cooking is not thought of as being on the light side, but this recipe is. Dutch oven cooking does not always have to involve cheese, beans, and meat. A very versatile cooking pot, it can be used for many different cooking methods, including stir-fry. Take care if cooking this recipe over campfire coals. The lid of the oven is not used, so if a wind comes up, a little ash may blow into your food.*

12	oz. cooked fettuccini or linguine	2	Tbsp. oil
3	boneless, skinless chicken breasts	2	Tbsp. olive oil
1	small can sliced olives	2	cloves minced garlic
3	chopped tomatoes	1	tsp. each of dried leaf basil and oregano, *or* 3 tsp. each of fresh
1	medium onion, sliced, then cut in half	2	Tbsp. balsamic vinegar
1	zucchini squash, sliced		¹/₄ to ¹/₂ tsp. cayenne pepper
1	small yellow squash, sliced		¹/₂ to ³/₄ cup fresh Parmesan cheese
			Salt and pepper to taste

Cut the chicken into one-inch cubes. With high bottom heat only (18-23 coals, or 450°), stir-fry the chicken in the oil. When the chicken is almost done, add both squashes, the garlic, and onion, and cook until tender. Then add the seasonings, vinegar, olives, olive oil and tomatoes and toss to mix; then toss in the pasta and Parmesan. Cook until the pasta is heated through. *Serves 6 to 8.*

Sweet & Spicy Chicken

8   boneless skinless chicken breasts (Other chicken pieces may be used, if desired. If using chicken pieces with the bone in, increase browning and cooking time.)
Cooking oil
1   large can pineapple chunks (do not drain the juice)
2   green peppers, cut into chunks
1   cup chicken broth
$^3/_4$ cup sugar
$^2/_3$ cup vinegar
2   tsp. soy sauce or more to taste
$^1/_2$ to 1 tsp. ground red pepper
Salt and pepper
$^1/_2$ tsp. garlic powder

Season the chicken with salt, pepper, and garlic powder, then brown in the Dutch oven with oil, turning it to brown all sides. Add the rest of the ingredients, including the juice from the canned pineapple. Cover and cook with 17 to 23 coals (425°), with a half-and-half ratio, for 30 to 35 minutes. Rotate the oven while cooking, and stir occasionally. Add more broth, if needed, while cooking. Sauce can be thickened with cornstarch and water if desired. *Serves 8.*

Turkey and Cornbread Stuffing Dinner

2   large turkey breasts
1   cup turkey or chicken broth
2   boxes of cornbread stuffing mix
$^1/_2$ lb. bulk sausage
$^1/_2$ cup diced celery
$^1/_2$ cup diced onion
$^1/_2$ cup shredded carrot
Salt, pepper, garlic, and poultry seasoning to taste

Oil the bottom and sides of the Dutch oven, then sprinkle the turkey breasts with seasonings and place them in the Dutch oven. Pour broth around the turkey, then cover and bake it in the Dutch oven with 17 to 23 coals (425°), with a 1 (bottom)-to-3 (top) ratio, for about 45 minutes to 1 hour, or until the turkey is done. Rotate the oven and lid while cooking, and add more broth if needed. While the turkey is cooking, prepare the stuffing. Brown the sausage in a saucepan or small Dutch oven. Stir the amount of water and butter called for in the stuffing mix into the sausage, then add the vegetables and seasoning packets from the stuffing mix. Cook until the vegetables are tender; then finish the stuffing as directed on the box. When the turkey is done, place the stuffing around the turkey, then cover and cook until the stuffing is slightly toasted on the top and sides (about 10 to 15 minutes). Slice the turkey and serve it with gravy or cranberry sauce, if desired. *Serves 5 to 7.*

☞ *Variation:* Use regular bread stuffing mix instead of the cornbread.

Turkey with Herbed Wild Rice

2   turkey breasts cut into cubes
2   6-oz. packages of fast-cooking wild rice
       with seasonings
1   small onion, diced
Hot water and butter as directed on rice package
$\frac{1}{2}$ cup additional butter
$\frac{1}{2}$ to 1 tsp. lemon juice
$\frac{1}{2}$ tsp. curry
2   cups frozen peas
Salt, lemon pepper, and garlic powder to taste

Brown the turkey, seasoned with salt, lemon pepper, and garlic, in a small amount of oil or butter. Add the rest of the ingredients except for the peas. (The recipe on the rice box will not ask for cold water, but never add cold water to a hot Dutch oven or it may crack.) Stir to make sure the ingredients are well mixed, then cover and cook with 16 to 20 coals (400°), with a half-and-half ratio, for 25 to 30 minutes or until the rice is soft. Stir occasionally, and add more moisture if needed. When the rice is done, stir in peas and cook for an additional 5 minutes. *Serves 5 to 6.*

Section Seven
Breakfasts

Blueberry and Cream Cheese Coffee Cake

2	packages of refrigerator crescent rolls	$1/2$	cup powdered sugar
1	package cream cheese	1	egg
1	tsp. vanilla	1	can blueberry pie filling

Oil the Dutch oven, then layer the crescent roll dough in the bottom of the oven (reserve 5 to 6 pieces to cut up and place on the top of the coffee cake). Mix the cream cheese, vanilla, powdered sugar, and egg together until smooth. Spread the cream-cheese mixture over the crescent roll dough, then spoon the blueberries over the cream-cheese mixture. Cut the reserved crescent roll dough into triangles and place it in a decorative pattern on top of the cream cheese. Cover and cook with 15 to 19 coals (375°), with a 1 (bottom)-to-3 (top) ratio, for 20 to 30 minutes. *Serves 8 to 10.*

Breakfast Hash

1	can corned beef	1	clove minced garlic
4 to 5	cups shredded hash browns		Salt, pepper, and seasoning salt to taste
1	onion, diced		Butter or oil for frying
$1/2$	green pepper, diced		

Heat the Dutch oven with 15 to 19 coals on the bottom only (375°). Cook the garlic, onion, and green pepper in a small amount of oil or butter in the Dutch oven, until almost tender. Add the hash browns and corned beef, then season to taste. Cook until the potatoes are browned. Add more oil or butter if needed during the cooking. Serve with hot sauce or salsa. *Serves 6.*

Breakfast Hash Browns with Bacon

1½ packages frozen hash browns
1   lb. cooked bacon (crumbled)
½   cup diced onion
½   cup diced green pepper
3   Tbsp. butter
1   can cream of chicken soup
½   tsp. salt
¼   tsp. pepper
Garlic powder to taste
1   cup grated cheese

Cook the green pepper and onion together in the butter, until tender. Mix the onion and green pepper with everything but the cheese, then place it in a greased Dutch oven. Cover and cook with 14 to 18 coals (350°), with a 1 (bottom)-to-2 (top) ratio, for 30 to 35 minutes or until the potatoes are browned. Sprinkle cheese on top and cook for 5 minutes more. *Serves 6.*

Breakfast in a Pot

8 to 10 sliced potatoes, scrubbed, with skins on
1   lb. bacon
1   lb. link sausage
1   green pepper, sliced thick
1   large onion, sliced thick
2   cans cream of mushroom soup
    mixed with 1 can of water
1 to 2 cups grated cheddar cheese
Salt, pepper, garlic powder, and seasoning salt to taste

Cook the bacon and sausage in the Dutch oven using 16 to 20 coals. Drain off all but about $^1/_4$ cup of the grease, then add the potatoes, onion and pepper. Stir, and season to taste. Pour the soup mixture over everything, then top it with cheese. Cover and cook with 16 to 22 coals (425°) for 30 to 40 minutes, or until the potatoes are tender. Rotate the lid and oven while cooking. Add more moisture if needed. *Serves 6 to 8.*

California Quiche

1   double ready-made pie
    crust package (the refrig-
    erated kind are easier to
    use when camping)
1   cup diced ham
2   cans diced green chilies
1   cup grated Swiss cheese

1   cup grated
    cheddar cheese
10 eggs, beaten
$^2/_3$ cup milk
$^1/_2$ tsp. salt
$^1/_4$ tsp. pepper

Oil the bottom of a 12-inch Dutch oven. Roll out the pie crust, combining both crusts to make one crust large enough to cover the Dutch oven and curve up the sides about 2 inches. Mix the rest of the ingredients and pour them into the pie crust. Do not let the eggs spill over the sides of the crust. Bake with 17 to 22 coals (425°), with 1 (bottom)-to-3 (top) ratio, for 30 to 35 minutes or until the egg is set. Serve with salsa and sour cream. *Serves 8 to 10.*

German Pancakes Dutch Style

☞ *This recipe was first cooked in a Dutch oven by my nephew Earl. He was about 16 years old at the time. He had already made these at home, and decided to try them in a Dutch oven. Needless to say, they turned out wonderfully.*

1   cup flour
1   cup milk
6   well-beaten eggs
1   cube melted butter (do not use margarine)

Mix half of the butter with the flour, eggs, and milk, and mix until smooth. Place the other half of the butter into the Dutch oven and rotate the oven to coat the side of the oven. Pour the batter in the oven, then cover and cook, using 18 to 23 coals (450°), with a 1 (bottom)-to-3 (top) ratio, for 20 to 25 minutes. Rotate the oven and lid while cooking. Serve hot with hot apple pie filling and powdered sugar or maple syrup. *Serves 4 to 6.*

One-Pot Breakfast

4   cups shredded hash browns
1   lb. bulk sausage
1½   cups grated cheese
10   eggs
⅔   cup milk
½   green pepper, diced fine
½   cup onion, diced fine
1   chopped tomato
½   tsp. salt
¼   tsp. pepper

Using 16 to 20 coals with bottom heat only, brown the sausage until it is almost done. Drain all but 2 to 3 tablespoons of fat from the oven, then add the hash browns, onion, and green pepper, and cook until the hash browns and sausage are well browned. In a mixing bowl, beat the eggs with milk, salt and pepper, and half of the cheese. Layer the chopped tomato over the hash browns and sausage mixture, then pour the egg-and-milk mixture over the top. Top with the rest of the cheese, and bake with a 1 (bottom)-to-3 (top) ratio, with 17 to 22 coals (425°), for 25 to 35 minutes or until the egg is set. Rotate the lid and oven while cooking. *Serves 8 to 10.*

Sticky Buns

1   package 24-count frozen bread rolls (thaw slightly)
1   small package butterscotch pudding mix (*not* instant)
$^1/_2$ cup brown sugar
$^2/_3$ cup melted butter
1   tsp. cinnamon
Chopped pecans or cashews (optional)

Mix the pudding mix, butter, brown sugar, cinnamon, and nuts together, using a whisk until smooth. Toss with the rolls in a large bowl, then pour into a well-oiled Dutch oven. Bake with 17 to 22 coals (425°), with 1 (top)-to-3 (bottom) ratio, for 30 to 40 minutes. Rotate the oven and lid while cooking. Turn out onto large platter when done. Serve hot. *Serves 12.*

Upside Down Apple Cinnamon Rolls

1   package large refrigerator cinnamon rolls
     (the pop-open kind, with icing)
2   apples (I prefer Granny Smith)
$1/2$ cup brown sugar
$1/4$ cup melted butter
$1/4$ cup chopped pecans (optional)

Cut a piece of cardboard the same size as the bottom of your Dutch oven and cover it with foil. Place it in the bottom of the oven, then spread a little oil on it. Peel, core, and chop the apples, then mix them with sugar, butter, and pecans. Spread the apples over the top of the foil, then place the cinnamon rolls on top. Bake with 16 to 20 coals (400°), with a 1 (bottom)-to-3 (top) ratio, for 25 to 30 minutes or until the rolls are done. Rotate the lid and oven while cooking. When done, turn out the cinnamon rolls onto a larger piece of cardboard covered with foil, or onto a large platter. The best way to do this is to place the platter on top of the oven, then very quickly turn the oven upside down. (Wear thick gloves when handling a hot oven.) Remove the cardboard piece from what is now the top of the rolls, and let them cool for a few minutes. Drizzle with the icing from the cinnamon-roll package and serve hot. *Makes 10 rolls.*

Section Eight

Desserts

Blueberry Tart

2   cans blueberry pie filling
1   refrigerator pie crust (for single pie only)
³/₄   cup flour
²/₃   cup sugar
¹/₂   tsp. cinnamon
¹/₂   cup of butter
¹/₂   cup pecans, chopped

Oil the bottom of a 12-inch Dutch Oven, then press the pie crust into the bottom of oven. Curve up the side of the oven if needed. Spread the blueberry filling over the crust. Mix the flour, sugar, cinnamon, and pecans together, then stir in the butter. Mix until the mixture is crumbly, then sprinkle on top of the blueberry filling. Cover and cook with 16 to 20 coals (400°), with a 1 (bottom)-to-3 (top) ratio, for 30 to 35 minutes. Rotate the oven and lid while cooking. *Serves 8 to 10.*

Candy Bar Cake

1   German chocolate cake mix,
     prepared as directed on the package
4 to 6 large candy bars (the kind with peanuts
     and caramel inside), chopped into large pieces
3/4   cup milk chocolate-chocolate chips
Whipped cream or ice cream

Mix the cake according to the package directions, then pour half of the batter into the oiled Dutch Oven. Cover and cook using 16 to 22 coals (400°), with 1 (bottom)-to-3 (top) ratio, for 15 minutes. After the cake has cooked for 15 minutes, remove it from the heat, then sprinkle the chopped candy bars and chocolate chips on top. Use care not to break the crust of the cooked cake. Then gently pour the rest of the cake mix over the top. Cover and return the oven to the heat, then cook for an additional 25 to 35 minutes or until the cake is done. Rotate the lid and oven while cooking and check often. Serve with whipped cream or ice cream. *Serves 8 to 12.*

Cherry Apple Crumble

4   apples, peeled, cored, and sliced, or chopped
      Mix with apples:
           $\frac{1}{2}$ cup sugar
           $\frac{1}{2}$ tsp. cinnamon
1   can cherry pie filling
10   graham crackers
1   cup brown sugar
$\frac{3}{4}$ cup rolled oats
$\frac{1}{2}$ cup flour
$\frac{3}{4}$ cup melted butter
$\frac{1}{2}$ tsp. each of nutmeg and all spice
1   tsp. cinnamon

Oil the Dutch oven, then line the bottom of the oven with the apple slices that have been mixed with the sugar and cinnamon, then spread the cherries over the top of the apples. Crumb the graham crackers very fine, then mix them with the other dry ingredients and spices. Drizzle melted butter over the crumb mixture, working the mixture with your hands until the butter is evenly distributed. Sprinkle the crumb topping on top of the cherries. Cover and cook with 16 to 20 coals (400°), with a 1 (bottom)-to-3 (top) ratio, for 30 to 35 minutes. Rotate the lid and oven while cooking. *Serves 8 to 10.*

Cranberry Apple Cobbler

1	16-oz. can whole cranberry sauce
5	apples, peeled, cored, and chopped
³/₄	cup brown sugar
2	Tbsp. flour
1	yellow cake mix
1	cup rolled oats
¹/₂	cup melted butter
1	egg

Combine the oats and cake mix together, then cut in the melted butter until the mixture is crumbly. Remove 1¹/₂ cups of the oats and cake mix mixture and reserve them for topping. Stir the egg into the remaining cake mixture, then press it into the bottom of the oiled Dutch oven. Mix the apples, brown sugar, flour, and cranberries together, then spread them over the cake mixture. Top with the reserved topping. Cover and cook with 15 to 17 coals (375°), with a 1 (bottom)-to-3 (top) ratio, for 30 to 40 minutes. Rotate the oven and lid while cooking. This is great with vanilla ice cream. *Serves 8 to 10.*

German Chocolate Turtle Cake

1   German chocolate cake mix,
      prepared as directed on package
16   oz. caramels
1/4   cup of butter
3/4   cup evaporated milk
3/4   cup pecans, chopped
1 1/2 cups milk chocolate-chocolate chips
Whipped cream or ice cream

Pour half of the cake batter into the bottom of an oiled Dutch oven. Cover and cook with 17 to 22 coals (400°), with a 1 (bottom)-to-3 (top) ratio, for 15 to 20 minutes, or until a soft crust forms on the top of the cake. While the cake is cooking, melt the caramels with butter and evaporated milk. When the cake has formed a crust, gently pour the caramel over the top (use care not to break through crust), then sprinkle the chocolate chips and pecans over the top. Pour the remaining cake batter over the top and bake for 25 to 35 minutes more, or until the cake is cooked through. Rotate the oven and lid while cooking and check the cake occasionally. Serve hot with whipped cream or ice cream. *Serves 8 to 10.*

Old Fashioned Peach Cobbler

Fruit base:

6   cups of fresh or preserved peaches, peeled and sliced
6   Tbsp. flour
1½ cups sugar (if using preserved peaches, use less sugar)
¼   tsp. nutmeg
1   tsp. lemon juice
4   Tbsp. butter

Mix together the peaches, sugar, nutmeg, lemon juice, and flour. Place in the bottom of a well-oiled Dutch Oven, then dot with pats of butter. Top with the Sweet Biscuit recipe below.

Sweet Biscuit topping:

2   cups flour
4   tsp. baking powder
½   tsp. salt
2   Tbsp. sugar
⅔   cup milk
½   cup shortening
½   tsp. cream of tarter

In a large bowl, mix the dry ingredients until blended, then cut in the shortening, a little at a time, until the mixture resembles coarse meal. Stir in the milk, then mix by hand just until the dough holds together. Do not over mix or the biscuits will not be flaky. Roll out the dough onto a floured surface to about $^1/_2$ to $^3/_4$ inch thickness. Cut with a biscuit cutter, then place them on top of the fruit base. Brush the tops of the biscuits with butter and sprinkle with a little sugar. Bake with 16 to 20 coals (375°), with a 1 (bottom)-to-3 (top) ratio, for 17 to 25 minutes. Rotate the lid and oven while cooking. Serve hot with ice cream or whipped cream. *Serves 8 to 10.*

Pumpkin Crumble

Crust and Crumb Topping:

1   package yellow cake mix
1   cup rolled oats
$^2/_3$ cup melted butter
1   egg
1   tsp. cinnamon
$^1/_2$ cup pecans, chopped

Filling:

1   large can pumpkin, pureed
3   eggs
1   cup brown sugar
1   can evaporated milk
1   tsp. cinnamon
1   Tbsp. pumpkin pie spice
$^1/_2$ tsp. salt

Mix the oats and cake mix together, then drizzle with butter and mix well until the butter is evenly mixed in. Reserve $1^1/_2$ cups of this mixture for a crumb topping. Add egg to the remaining cake mix, then press it into the bottom of an oiled Dutch Oven. Mix together the filling ingredients until smooth, then pour them over the top of the cake mixture. Mix the reserved cake mix with cinnamon and pecans, then sprinkle it over the top of the pumpkin mix. Cover and cook with 16 to 22 coals (375°) for about 45 minutes to 1 hour. Rotate the oven and lid while cooking and check often. *Serves 8 to 12.*

Spiced Apple Raisin Crumb Cake

1	spice cake mix	³/₄	cup sugar
1	cup rolled oats	¹/₂	tsp. cinnamon
4	apples, peeled, cored, and sliced thin	¹/₄	tsp. allspice
		1	egg
1	cup raisins	²/₃	cup melted butter

Combine the cake mix and oats, then cut in the melted butter and mix until crumbly. Save 1¹/₂ cups of this mixture for topping. Add the egg to the rest of the cake mix and oats and mix well. Press the mixture into the bottom of a well-oiled Dutch oven. Mix the apples, raisins, sugar, cinnamon and allspice together, then spread this over the cake and oat mixture. Sprinkle the reserved topping on top. Bake with 17 to 22 coals (425°), with a 1 (bottom)-to-3 (top) ratio, for 30 to 35 minutes. *Serves 8 to 10.*

Toffee Cake

1   German chocolate cake mix, prepared as directed on package
1   can sweetened, condensed milk
1   small jar butterscotch topping
5 to 6 crushed toffee candy bars
Whipped cream or ice cream

Mix the cake mix and cook it in an oiled Dutch oven with 17 to 22 coals (425°), with a 1 (bottom)-to-3 (top) ratio, for 30 to 40 minutes or until done. While the cake is cooking, crush the toffee bars and mix the condensed milk and butterscotch together. When the cake is done, remove it from the heat and poke holes half way through the cake with the end of a wooden spoon. Pour the butterscotch mixture over the cake, then top it with the crushed candy bars. Serve with whipped cream or ice cream. *Serves 8 to 10.*

Upside-Down Tropical Delight

1   package of the grand-sized
     refrigerator buttermilk biscuits
²/₃   cup melted butter
1   small can crushed pineapple, drained
1   cup coconut
³/₄   cup of brown sugar
2   Tbsp. flour
¹/₄   tsp. all spice

Mix the flour, sugar and all spice together, then add the coconut and pineapple. Drizzle with butter, and mix it until well blended. Spread this mixture onto the bottom of an oiled Dutch oven. Place the biscuits on top, then cover and cook with 16 to 22 coals (400°), at a 1 (bottom)-to-3 (top) ratio, for 25 to 30 minutes or until the biscuits are golden brown. Serve with whipped cream. *Serves 8 to 10.*

Section Nine

Group Cooking

Cooking for Crowds

Cooking for a large group can be extremely stressful. It is difficult to decide how much food to buy. If you buy too much you are eating it for months, but if you buy too little you feel as though some guests may have gone without. Below is a chart designed to alleviate some of the guesswork involved in cooking for a group. Note that two small children (under the age of eight) will probably count as one adult.

Meats	25 servings	50 servings	100 servings
Hot dogs	6 to 7 lbs.	13 lbs.	25 lbs.
Hamburger	9 to 10 lbs.	18 lbs.	35 lbs.
Chicken	13 to 15 lbs.	25 to 30 lbs.	50 to 65 lbs.

Note: Chicken with bones will serve fewer people per pound than boneless chicken.

	25 servings	50 servings	100 servings
Turkey	15 to 16 lbs.	27 to 30 lbs.	55 to 65 lbs.
Boneless roast beef	13 to 15 lbs.	27 to 35 lbs.	55 to 65 lbs.
Roast with bone	25 lbs.	50 lbs.	100 lbs.
Boneless ribs	12 to 13 lbs.	25 to 27 lbs.	50 to 55 lbs.
Ribs with bone	25 lbs.	50 lbs.	100 lbs.

Vegetables, salads, and casseroles

	25 servings	50 servings	100 servings
Lettuce for green salad	4 heads	8 heads	16 heads
Mashed potatoes	10 to 12 lbs.	20 to 24 lbs.	40 to 45 lbs.
Baked beans	1 gallon	2 gallons	4 gallons

	25 servings	**50 servings**	**100 servings**
Jell-O salad	³/₄ gallon	1¹/₂ gallons	2¹/₄ gallons
Tomatoes, sliced	3 to 5 lbs.	7 to 10 lbs.	14 to 17 lbs.
Potato salad	1¹/₂ gallons	2¹/₂ gallons	4¹/₂ gallons
Potatoes (uncooked)	12 to 13 lbs.	25 lbs.	50 lbs.
Carrots	6¹/₄ lbs.	12¹/₂ lbs.	25 lbs.

Miscellaneous

	25 servings	50 servings	100 servings
Watermelon	37 lbs.	75 lbs.	150 lbs.
Mixed fruit or cocktail	3 quarts	6 quarts	12 quarts
Whipped cream	1 pint	2 pints	3 pints
Ice cream	³/₄ gallon	1¹/₂ gallons	3 gallons
Butter	³/₄ lb.	1¹/₂ lbs.	3 lbs.
Rolls	4 doz.	8 doz.	16 doz.
Bread	3 loaves	6 loaves	12 loaves
Crackers	1¹/₂ lbs.	3 lbs.	6 lbs.
Cheese	3 lbs.	6 lbs.	12 lbs.
Soup	1¹/₂ gallons	3 gallons	6 gallons
Soup as main dish	2¹/₂ gallons	5 gallons	10 gallons
Salad dressings	1 pint	2 pints	4 pints
Coffee or tea	¹/₂ lb.	1 lb.	2 lbs.

Number of 12-inch Dutch ovens needed

	25 servings	50 servings	100 servings
Baked beans (full)	1 oven	2 ovens	4 ovens
Potatoes and onions	2 ovens	4 ovens	8 ovens
Stew	2 ovens	4 ovens	8 ovens
Cobbler or desserts	3 ovens	5 ovens	10 ovens

	25 servings	50 servings	100 servings
Boneless ribs	2 ovens	4 ovens	7 ovens
Ribs with bones	3 ovens	5 ovens	10 ovens
Chicken, boneless	2 ovens	4 ovens	7 ovens
Chicken with bones	3 ovens	6 ovens	10 ovens
Casserole-Type Dishes	3 ovens	5 ovens	10 ovens

When cooking for large numbers, propane cookers designed especially for Dutch ovens work best by far. Cooking with charcoal is just as effective, but will take far more time and effort. If cooking with charcoal, ovens can be stacked on top of each other during cooking. The coals on the lid of the bottom oven will supply the oven on top of it with its bottom heat. Place the largest oven on the bottom, then work your way up, going down in size. Do not stack more than four ovens high.

When cooking for groups of 50 or more, it is wise to assign people to different areas. Put one person in charge of starting and keeping charcoal going, one on desserts, one on meat, and so on. It also is a good idea to have one or two people to help anyone who is running behind or to do odd jobs such as opening cans or cutting up vegetables. If cooking for 100 or more people, assign two or three people per station. These people can also help you serve the food to the guests.

Advanced preparation (or the lack of it) can make or break the process of cooking for a large crowd. Plan ahead, and never leave everything for the last minute. If meat needs to be cut or cubed, do it ahead of time and store it in zip-lock baggies. Vegetables can be cut up ahead of time and stored in them also. (If cutting up potatoes ahead of time, cover them with water to keep them from browning.) Sauces can even be mixed ahead and stored in containers with tight-fitting lids. Make sure all equipment is clean and in good working order before the dinner. You cannot pull out a rusty Dutch oven which has not been used for several years and expect to cook in it that way. Make sure all the ovens are clean and seasoned well in advance.

Many of the recipes in this book can easily be doubled or tripled to feed even larger crowds. Follow the chart to help you decide how many times you need to multiply the ingredients. The recipes in this section are easy recipes that multiply well and take little prep time.

Beef with Biscuits

☞ *This is a complete meal in one pot that everyone will love.*

1¹/₂ lbs. ground beef
2   cloves minced garlic
1   large can kidney beans
1   can kernel corn
1   large onion diced
2   cans tomato soup
¹/₂   tsp. chili powder
¹/₄   tsp. oregano
¹/₄   tsp. cumin
1   package grand sized pop open type buttermilk biscuits
1¹/₂ cups grated cheddar cheese

Brown the ground beef with onion and garlic, using 16 to 20 coals with bottom heat only. Stir in the soup, corn, beans, and seasonings. Place the biscuits on top, then cover and cook at 375 degrees, with a 1 (bottom)-to-2 (top) ratio, for 18 to 22 minutes or until the biscuits are golden brown and cooked through. Sprinkle cheese on top and cook until the cheese melts.

Chicken and Potatoes

☞ *This was the first Dutch oven meal we ever cooked. For the first year we were afraid to cook anything else. We camped almost every weekend so we ate chicken and potatoes almost every weekend. We are finally back to where we like this dish again after eating it so many times.*

4 to 6 boneless, skinless chicken breasts
Flour (about 1 cup) seasoned with salt, pepper,
    garlic powder, and seasoning salt
8 to 12 sliced potatoes (with or without skins)
1 to 2 large onions, sliced
½   lb. bacon cut into 1-inch pieces
2   cans cream of mushroom soup
1   can of cola, or lemon-lime soda
Grated cheese
Additional salt, pepper, garlic powder, and seasoning salt

Fry the bacon in the Dutch oven until crisp, then remove it from the oven. Leave the bacon grease in the oven (the bacon can be placed on turned up lid of Dutch oven until needed). While the bacon is cooking, dredge the chicken breasts in the seasoned flour. Cook the chicken in the bacon grease until well browned, turning it to cook both sides, then remove it from the oven. Drain and save the grease from the oven, then layer the potatoes, seasonings, onions, bacon, and cheese in the Dutch oven, ending with a layer of cheese. Mix together the cream of mushroom soup and the soda. Drizzle the potatoes with bacon grease (desired amount), then place the chicken on top of the potatoes. Pour the mushroom-soup mixture over the top. Cover and cook, with 17 to 22 coals (425°), with a half-and-half ratio, for 30 to 45 minutes or until the potatoes are tender. Rotate the oven and lid while cooking, and add more moisture if needed. *Serves 4 to 6.*

Chili Dogs

☞ *This recipe is great for Boy Scout troops or really casual get-togethers. Everyone chooses his own toppings for the chili dogs and has fun putting them together.*

Hot dogs, 1 or 2 per person
Hot dog buns, 1 or 2 per person (toasted buns taste best)
Canned chili, one 16-oz. can will top 2 to 3 hot dogs

Place the chili and hot dogs together in the Dutch oven and cook them with bottom heat only (15 to 19 coals, or 375°), until both are heated through, about 15 to 20 minutes. Place the hot dogs on toasted buns, and top with the chili and any or all of the garnish ingredients below.

Garnishes:
    Diced onion
    Grated cheese
    Crushed tortilla chips
    Jalapeño pepper rings
    Salsa
    Sour cream

Complete Barbecue Dinner

☞ *Great when serving a lot of people. It is very easy to pre-pare and a real crowd pleaser.*

Meat: chicken, beef or pork, about ½ lb.
    per person if boneless, or 1 lb. each with bones.
Sliced potatoes, 1 to 2 per person
Sliced onions, about ¼ per person
Baby carrots, about ½ cup per person
Diced celery, ½ stalk per person
Bottled barbecue sauce
Oil for browning meat
Salt and pepper

Season the meat with salt and pepper, then brown it in a small amount of oil, working in batches if necessary. Cook it until the meat is well browned, then add the rest of the ingredients to the oven. Pour the barbecue sauce over the top, then toss to coat everything with the sauce. Cover and cook with 17 to 23 coals (425°), for 40 to 45 minutes, or until the meat is tender and the potatoes are soft.

Corn Dogs

☞ *A great recipe for Scouts because it can easily be doubled or tripled and almost every kid likes corn dogs. Use a lot of care in cooking these with Scouts, allow only adults to cook with hot oil.*

1   cup corn meal
1   cup flour
2   tsp. baking powder
1   Tbsp. prepared mustard
1   Tbsp. chili powder
2   eggs
1¼   cup milk
1½   tsp. salt
1   Tbsp. sugar
1   package 10-count hot dogs
10   corn-dog sticks or Popsicle sticks

Mix everything but the hot dogs with a wire whip until smooth. Heat oil in the oven with bottom heat only, heating to between 325 to 375 degrees. Insert the sticks into the hot dogs, then dip them in the batter and fry them a few at a time until deep golden brown, turning them as needed. Remove them from the oil with a slotted spoon or skimmer, and place them on paper towels to drain. This batter is also great for onion rings or fried zucchini. *Makes 10 corndogs.*

Dutch Oven Fajitas

☞ *A fast and easy meal, easily done for large crowds.*

2 lbs. of boneless, skinless chicken breasts or sirloin steak,
   or a combination of both cut into strips and marinated
   overnight in the following:
   - $1/2$ cup bottled sweetened lime juice
   - 3   Tbsp. liquid smoke
   - 2   cloves minced garlic
   - $1/4$ cup of oil
   - $1/4$ tsp. ground red pepper

1 to 2 large onions
1   red bell pepper
1   green bell pepper
1   yellow bell pepper
Salt and pepper to taste
Oil for frying

Heat the oil in the Dutch oven over bottom heat (15 to 19
coals, or 375°), then stir-fry the meat, onions and bell peppers
until the meat is done and the peppers and onions are tender.
Serve rolled up in warm tortillas, with the garnishes listed
below. *Serves 4 to 6.*

Garnish

Fajita-style flour tortillas   Fresh salsa
Grated cheese   Shredded lettuce
Sour cream   Chopped tomatoes
Guacamole

Easy One-Pot Spaghetti

1½   lbs. ground beef
2   cloves of minced garlic
1   large onion, diced
1   large jar spaghetti sauce
8   oz. uncooked spaghetti noodles
1   cup of water (or more as needed)
1   lb. sliced mushrooms
1   green pepper (optional)
½   tsp. ground basil
½   tsp. cinnamon
¼   tsp. ground red pepper

Brown the ground beef with garlic and onion in the Dutch oven. Stir in the rest of the ingredients, then cover and cook with 17 to 22 coals (425°), with a half-and-half ratio, for 25 to 30 minutes or until the noodles are tender. Stir occasionally, and add more water if needed. *Serves 6 to 8.*

Hawaiian Pork Chops

3/4   cup Italian salad dressing
1   large can pineapple chunks (do not drain the juice)
1/2 to 3/4 cup brown sugar
4   Tbsp. soy sauce
Salt, pepper, and garlic powder to taste
8   pork chops
Hot cooked rice
Water & cornstarch to thicken the sauce if desired

Brown the pork chops in the Dutch oven using 16 to 20 coals. Mix together the juice from the pineapple, the brown sugar, Italian dressing and soy sauce in a small bowl and whisk until smooth, then pour it over the pork chops. Add the pineapple, then cover and cook, using 16 to 19 coals (375°), with 1 (bottom)-to-2 (top) ratio, for 35 to 45 minutes or until the chops are tender. *Serves 4 to 8.*

One-Pot Spanish Chicken with Rice

6   boneless, skinless chicken breasts
2   packages of Spanish rice mix
     (the brand that calls for whole tomatoes)
2   14-oz cans of whole tomatoes (do no drain)
Water as directed on the rice mix
Butter as directed on the rice mix
Diced green onions
Chopped tomatoes
Grated cheddar cheese
Oil for frying

Fry the chicken in a Dutch oven with a small amount of oil, using 16 to 20 coals. When the chicken is done, remove it from the oven. Slowly add the rice, the seasoning mix that comes with the rice, whole tomatoes with juice (chopped slightly to break them into smaller pieces), water, and butter, then stir to mix. Place the chicken on top of the rice, cover and cook with 17 to 23 coals (425°), with a half-and-half ratio, for 25 to 30 minutes or until the rice is tender. Rotate the lid and oven while cooking, and add more moisture if needed. Try not to stir while cooking, but if needed, rice can be gently lifted to rotate. When the rice is done, top with cheese, tomatoes, and onions, then cover it again and cook until the cheese is melted and the tomatoes are hot. Serve with sour cream if desired. *Serves 6.*

One-Pot Stroganoff

1   lb. sirloin steak, cut into strips
4   cups of curly pasta
1   onion
2   cloves of minced garlic
1   lb. sliced mushrooms
3   Tbsp. Worcestershire sauce
1½ cups beef broth
2   cans tomato soup
Salt and pepper to taste
1½ cups sour cream

Cook the steak with onion and garlic until it is browned. Add the mushrooms, pasta, beef broth, Worcestershire sauce, soup, salt and pepper to taste. Cover and cook with 17 to 23 coals (425°), with 1 (bottom)-to-3 (top) ratio, for 30 to 35 minutes, or until the noodles are done. Add more broth or hot water, if needed, while cooking. When the noodles are done, stir in the sour cream and serve hot. *Serves 6 to 8.*

Sloppy Joe's

2   lbs. ground beef
1   small bottle smoky flavored barbecue sauce
3   Tbsp. prepared mustard
1   cup ketchup
$^1/_2$ to $^3/_4$ cup brown sugar
2   onions diced
2   cloves minced garlic
3   Tbsp. Worcestershire sauce
Salt, pepper, and ground red pepper to taste

Using 16 to 19 coals with bottom heat only (about 375 degrees), cook the ground beef with onion and garlic in the Dutch oven until it is cooked through. Stir in the rest of the ingredients, cover and cook, moving the coals to a half-and-half ratio, for 20 to 25 minutes. Serve hot on hamburger buns. *Serves around 12.*

Tacos in a Bowl

2   lbs. hamburger
1   diced onion
1   large can diced tomatoes
1   5-oz. can kidney beans
1   packet taco seasoning
2   8 oz cans tomato sauce
1   to 2 cups water
1   small can sliced olives
½   tsp. cumin

Brown the hamburger and onion in the Dutch oven using 16 to 20 coals. Add the rest of the ingredients, then cover and simmer, stirring occasionally for 15 to 20 minutes with 15 to 19 coals (375°). Heat can be from the bottom only, or from half on top and half on the bottom. Spoon into bowls, then top with desired toppings from the list below. *Serves about 6 to 8.*

Toppings
Tortilla chips
Grated cheese
Salsa
Diced tomatoes
Diced onion
Sour cream

About the Author

I grew up in the small northern Utah town of Fielding, population about 400. I am the youngest of six children born to my parents, Gordon and Doris Smith. My mother is a wonderful cook and I owe any cooking talents I may have to her. My family loves to camp and loves to cook, so I guess I was destined to be introduced to Dutch oven cooking.

Since I can remember, I have always enjoyed cooking outdoors. I remember making mud pies with my cousins, and mine always had to have some sort of a decoration or filling of leaves or berries of some sort. Before long I had branched out into mud tacos and mud burgers. I was the Queen of cooking with mud. (Thus came the nickname *Mud Pie Marla*) These were my first outdoor cooking experiences, and you're probably glad to know that I have come a long way since then.

My husband and I received a Dutch oven as a wedding present from my parents. For the first year we cooked nothing but Dutch oven chicken and potatoes because we didn't dare try anything else. We camped almost every weekend so we were getting really tired of chicken and potatoes. We soon learned that a Dutch oven was more forgiving than we thought and began experimenting. Before long, we were enjoying Dutch oven pizza, stir fry, and countless other dishes.

I was introduced to Camp Chef, a company out of Logan Utah, that manufactures and sells outdoor cookers designed for

Dutch oven cooking and other types of outdoor cooking. They have attachments for barbecue grilling and griddle frying, just to name a few. I became very interested in their company because it really simplified my Dutch oven cooking and it also expanded my options for outdoor cooking. The end result was that I wrote a cook book titled *Camp Chef Outdoor Cooking Guide*, designed especially to go with the products they sell.

Since then I have cooked at retailer grand openings, anniversary sales and countless other outdoor events. My second book was *Favorite Utah Pioneer Recipes*, published by Horizon Publishers.

I now reside with my husband and three children in North Ogden, Utah, and one of our favorite things to do is enjoy the great outdoors.

Recipes are guides, not rules, so use your creativity and don't let outdoor cooking intimidate you. And whatever you do, don't eat chicken and potatoes for a year like we did.